RECORDED VERSIONS GUITAR

AUTHENTIC TRANSCRIPTIONS WITH NOTES AND TABLATURE

BEST OF ROBERT CRAY

Cover photo courtesy of Robert Cray

Music transcriptions by Addi Booth, Jeff Jacobson, Bill LaFleur, Ron Piccione, and David Stocker

ISBN 978-1-4803-8788-1

HAL•LEONARD®
CORPORATION

7777 W. BLUEMOUND RD. P.O. BOX 13819 MILWAUKEE, WI 53213

In Australia Contact:
Hal Leonard Australia Pty. Ltd.
4 Lentara Court
Cheltenham, Victoria, 3192 Australia
Email: ausadmin@halleonard.com.au

T005761 7

Visit Hal Leonard Online at
www.halleonard.com

from *Shoulda Been Home*
Baby's Arms
Words and Music by Robert Cray

way too long.　　　But I'll be there with you　soon as we get　off the phone.　I'm go-in' home.

Pre-Chorus

I'm go-in' home.

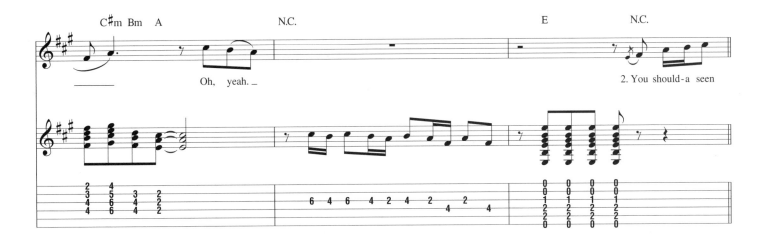

Oh, yeah.　　　　　　　　　　　　　　　　2. You should-a seen

Verse

me　　　　　　　pack last night.　　　　Read-in' ev-'ry

Pre-Chorus

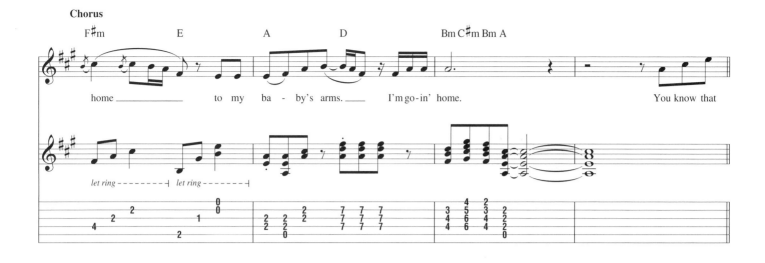

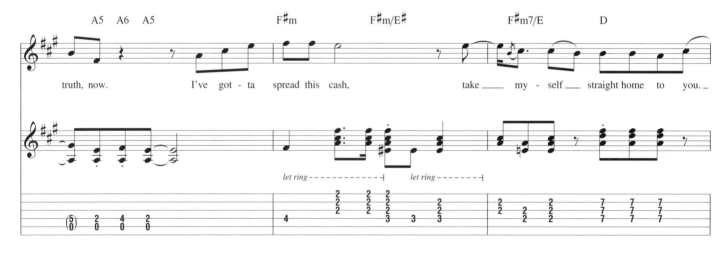

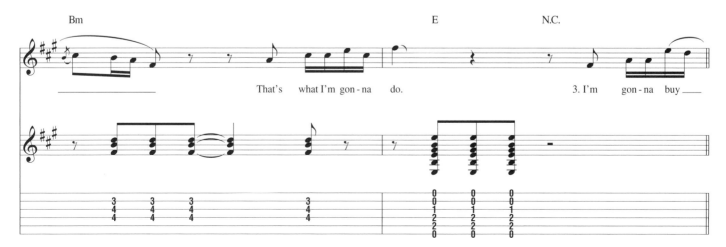

Verse

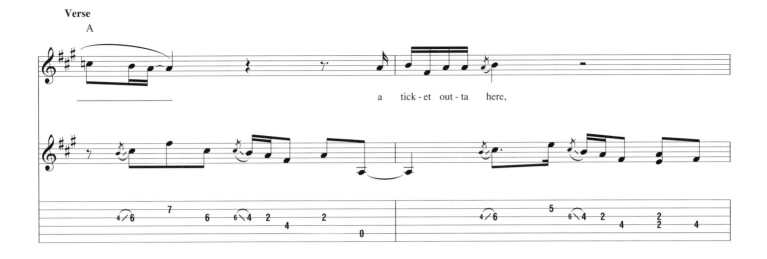

a tick-et out-ta here,

get on _____ back to my _____ ba - by's arms. _____ There ain't a

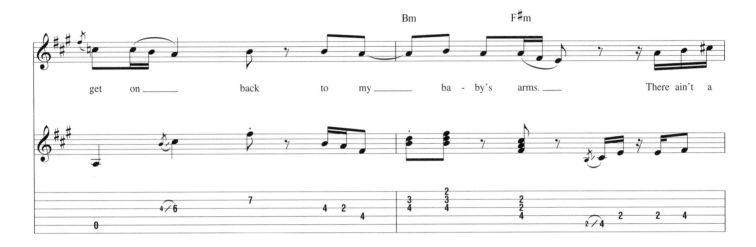

thing or no-bod-y gon-na get in my way. I'll be on the

first thing smok-in', _____ man, _____ lat-er on to-day. I'm go-in'

6

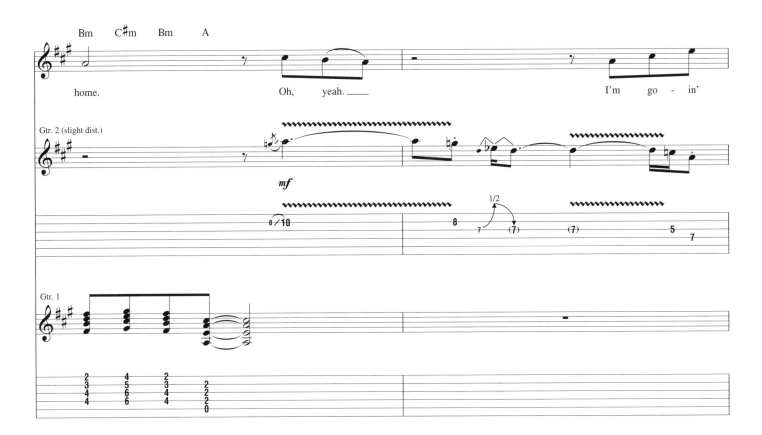

8

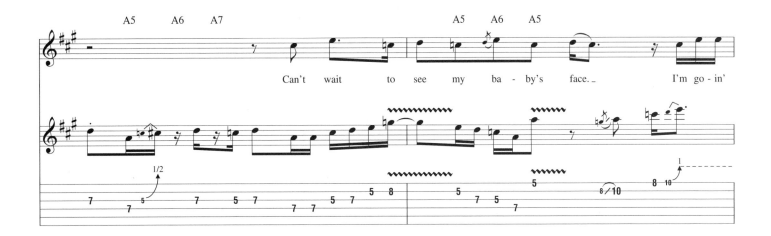

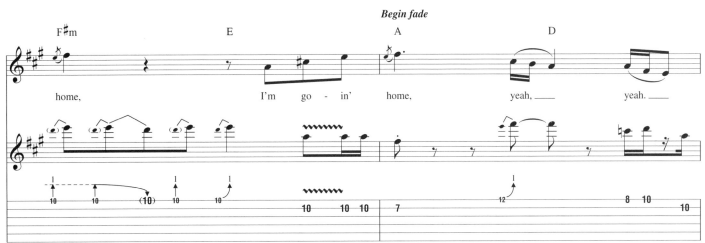

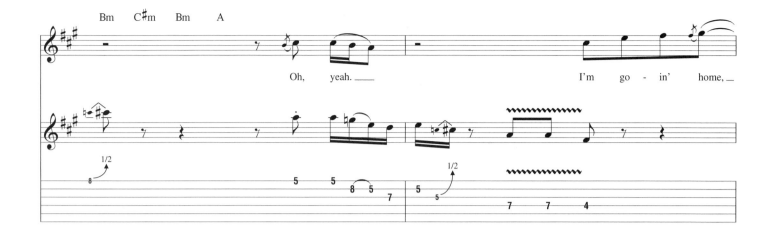

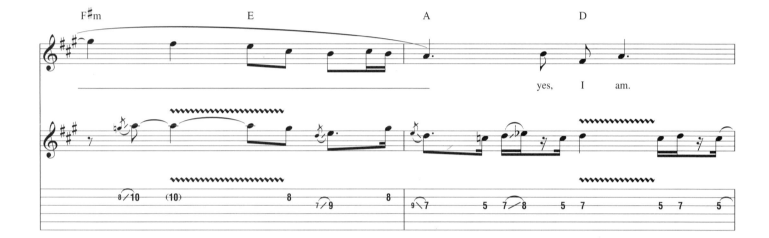

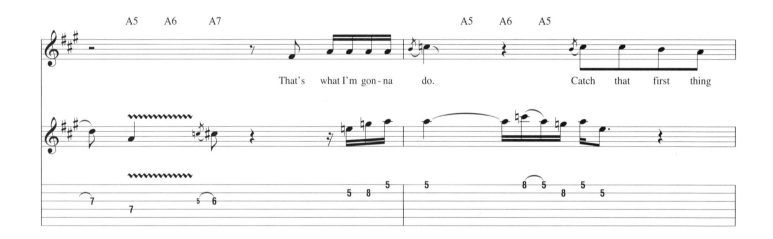

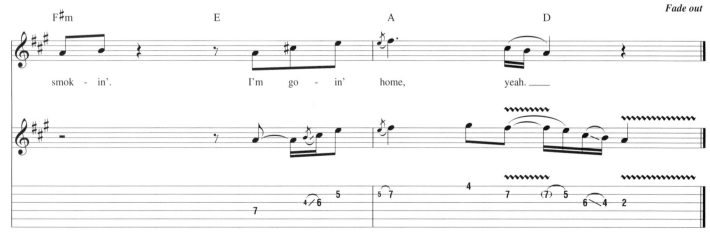

Bad Influence

Words and Music by Robert Cray and Michael Vannice

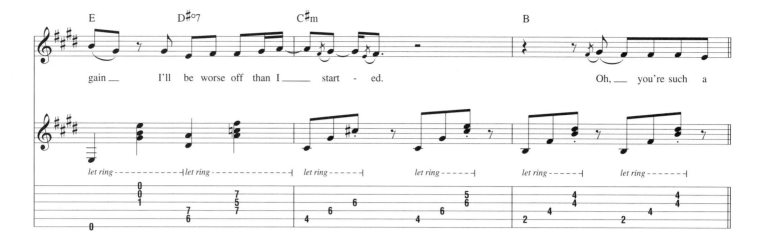

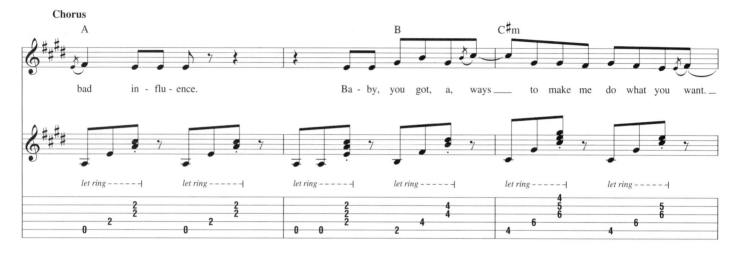

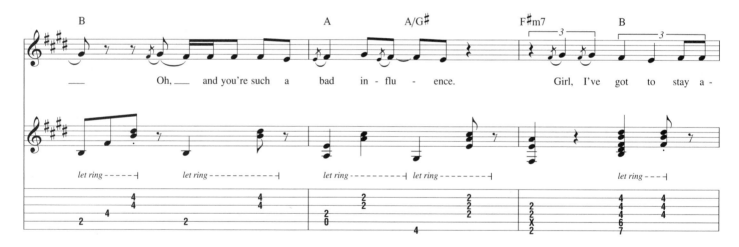

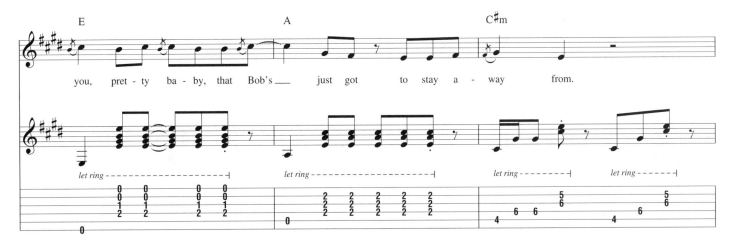

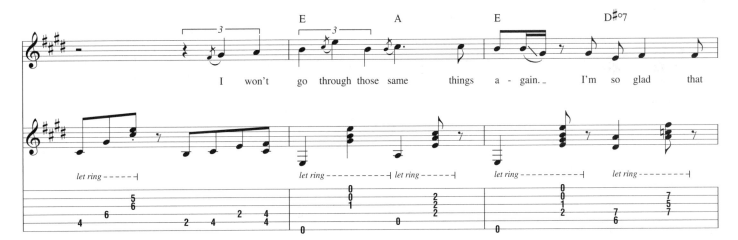

Ba - by, you've got, a, ways ___ to make me do what you want. ___ Oh, ___ and you're such a

bad in - flu - ence. Girl, I've got to stay a - way.

Saxophone Solo

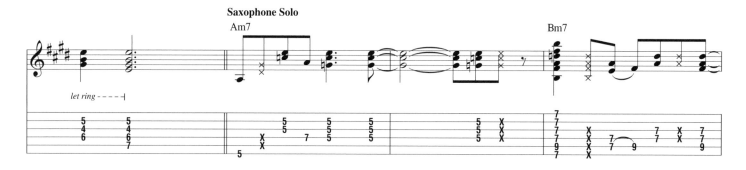

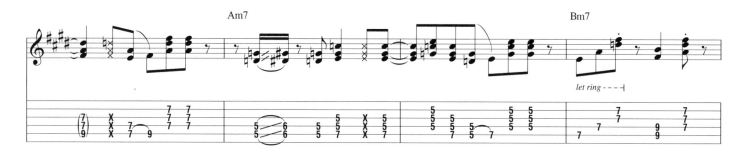

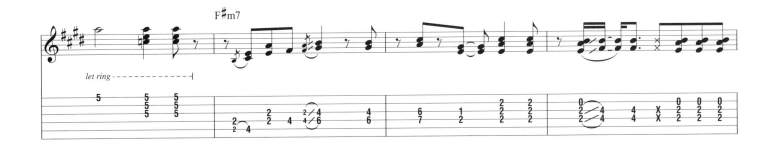

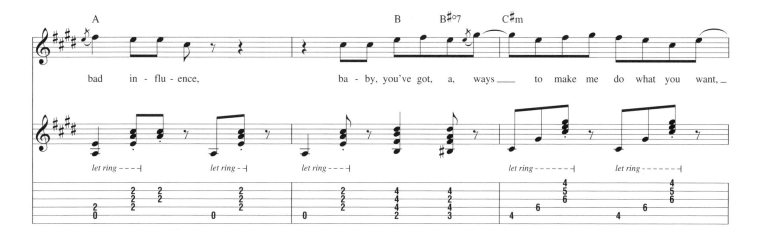

bad in-flu-ence, ba - by, you've got, a, ways___ to make me do what you want,___

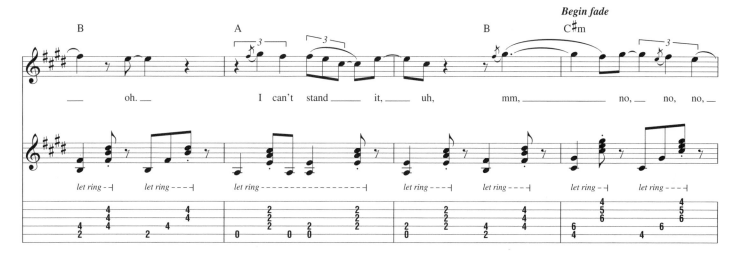

___ oh. ___ I can't stand ___ it, ___ uh, mm, ___ no, ___ no, no, ___

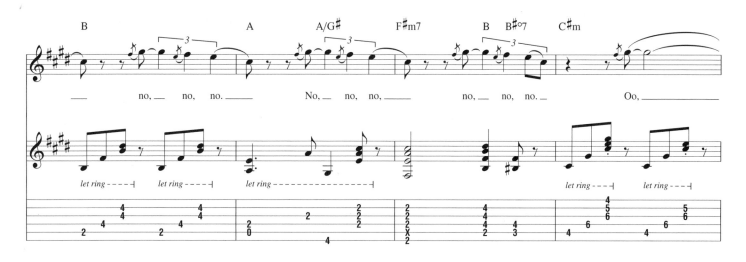

___ no, ___ no, no. No, ___ no, no, ___ no, ___ no, no. ___ Oo, ___

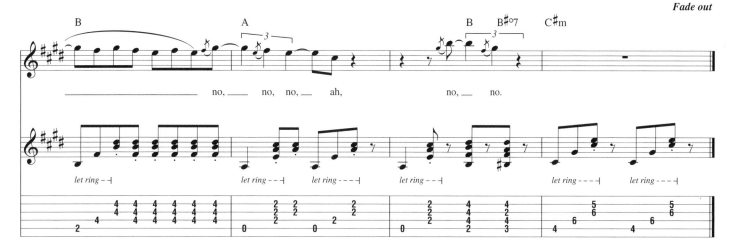

___ no, ___ no, no, ___ ah, no, ___ no.

(Won't Be) Coming Home

Words and Music by Hendrix Ackle and Richard Cousins

Verse

Gtr. 2 tacet

1. As her car pulls out __ the drive - way   and she don't wave __ good - bye,

her last words __ ech - o in my mind; __

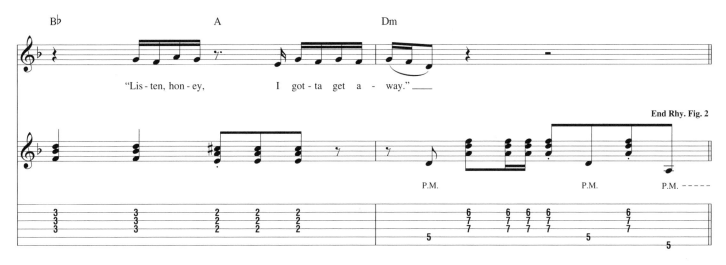

"Lis - ten, hon - ey,   I got - ta get a - way." __

Verse

Chorus

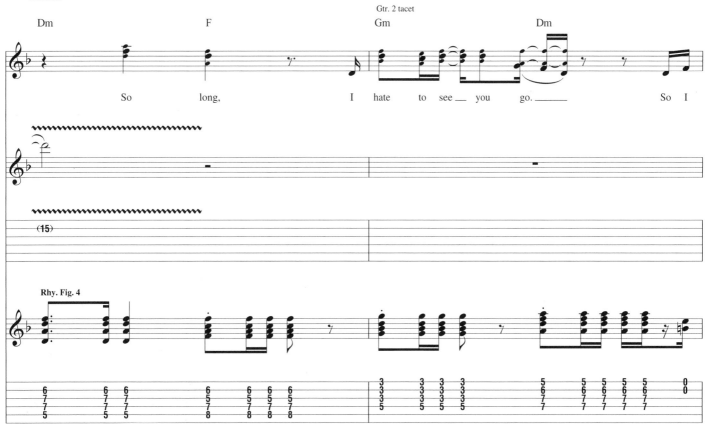

So long, I hate to see you go. So I

save my tears for lat-er on down the road. How come I

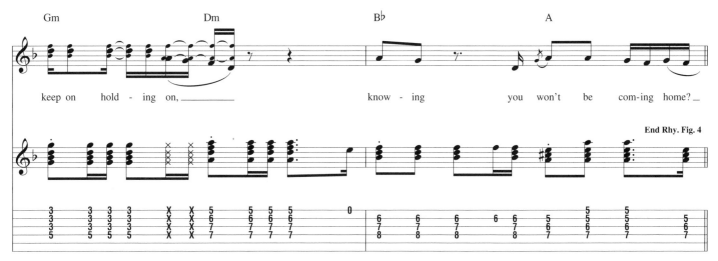

keep on hold-ing on, know-ing you won't be com-ing home?

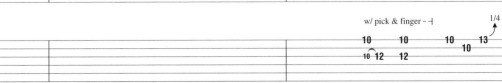

Chorus

Gtr. 1: w/ Rhy. Fig. 4

So long, I hate to see you go. But I'll save my tears for lat-er on down the road.

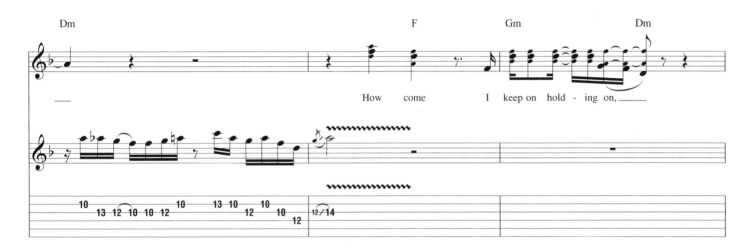

How come I keep on hold-ing on,

Gtr. 1: w/ Rhy. Fig. 3 (1st 2 meas.)

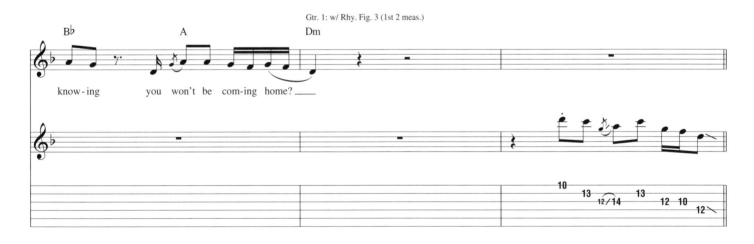

know-ing you won't be com-ing home?

Bridge

Gtr. 2 tacet

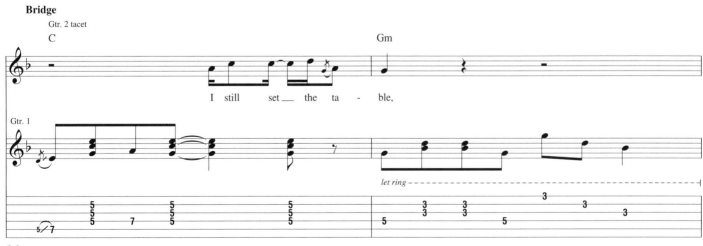

I still set the ta-ble,

Gtr. 1

let ring

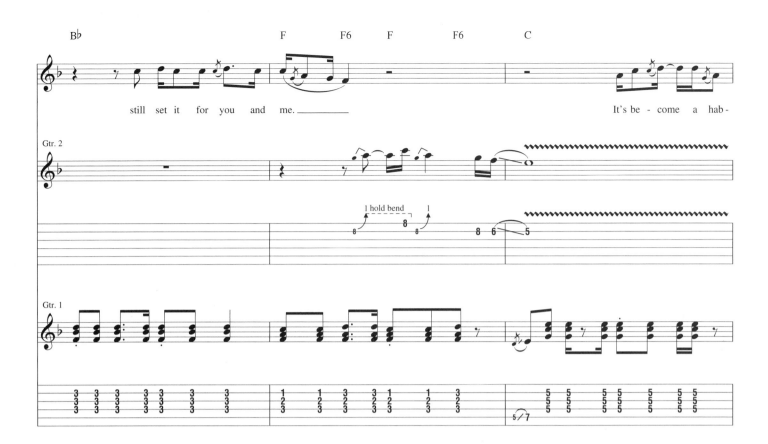

still set it for you and me. _____ It's be - come a hab -

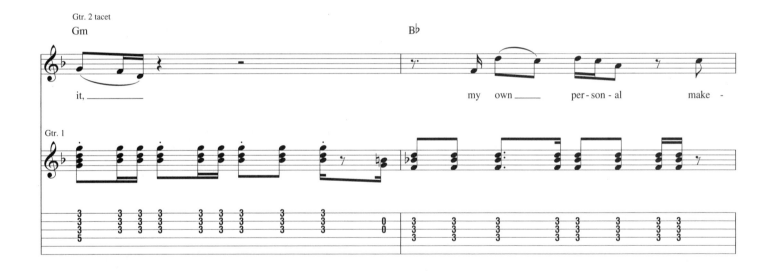

it, _____ my own _____ per - son - al make -

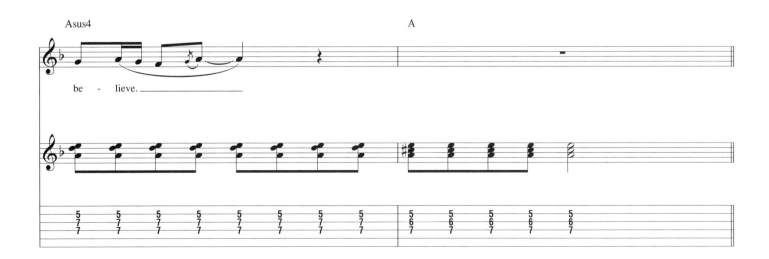

be - lieve. _____

Guitar Solo

Gtr. 1 tacet

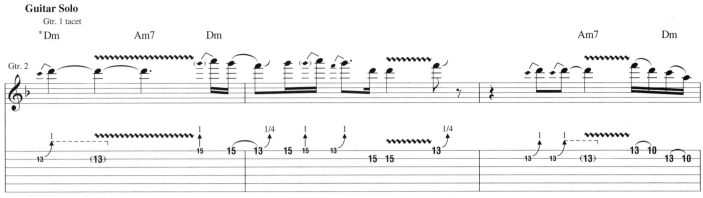

*Chord symbols reflect overall harmony.

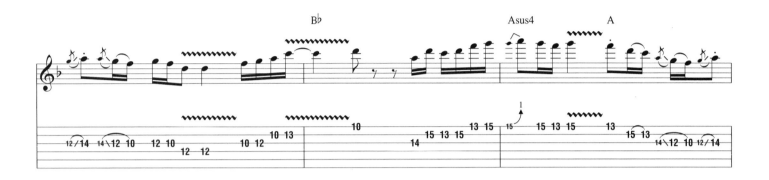

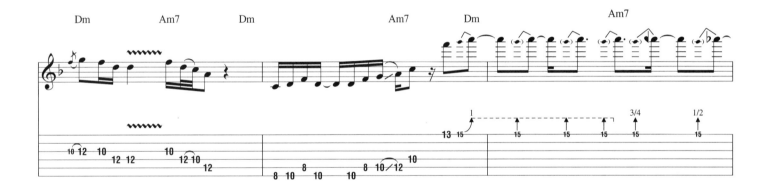

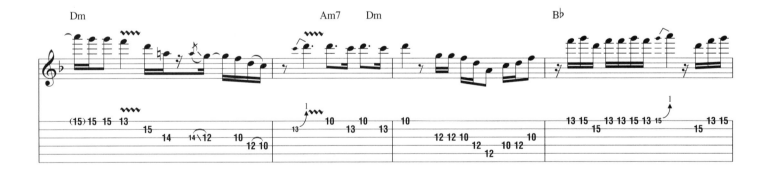

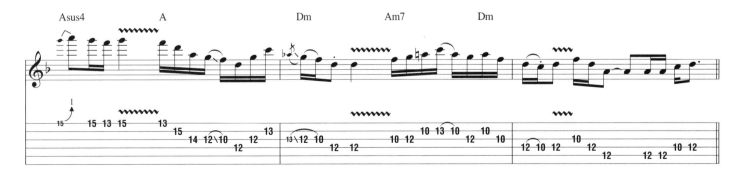

Chorus

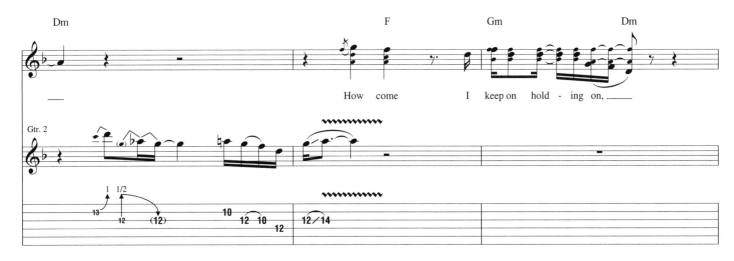

Chorus

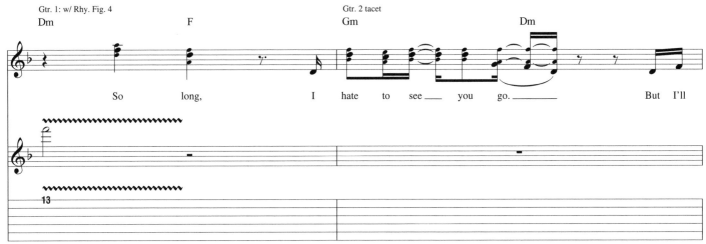

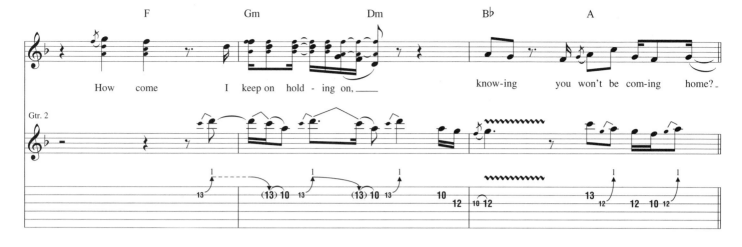

How come I keep on hold - ing on, ____ know-ing you won't be com-ing home? _

Gtr. 2

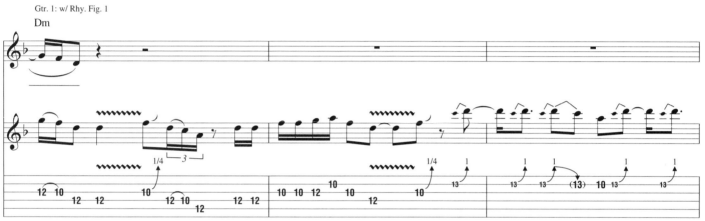

Outro-Guitar Solo

Gtr. 1: w/ Rhy. Fig. 1

Gtr. 1: w/ Rhy. Fig. 2 (1st 2 meas.)

You won't be com-ing home. ____

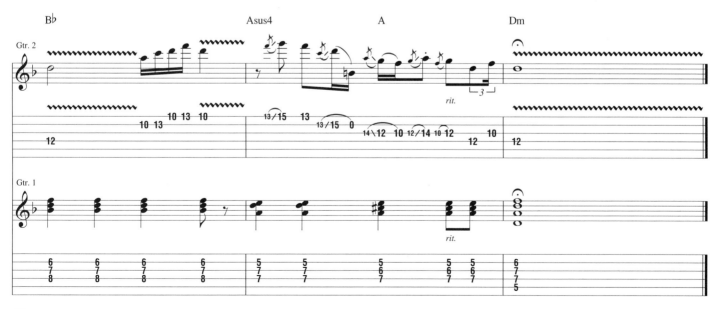

Gtr. 2

Gtr. 1

Don't Be Afraid of the Dark

Words and Music by Dennis L. Walker

1. Dead of night, ba - by, we're
2. It might get scar - y
3. You might trem - ble,

fi - nal - ly ___ a - lone. ___
'til your eyes ___ ad - just.
you might shake.

I'll pull down the shades ___ if you'll un - plug this phone. ___
Don't fear the shad - ows, in me you can trust. ___ I'm
Scream out ___ loud, ___ you may e - ven pray. ___ I ___

Put on some mu - sic, Mar - vin Gaye's ___ re al ___ nice.
___ at ___ my best in a pitch black room. ___
___ know which moves suit you right.

Once we get set - tled I'll turn out the lights. ___
Hold on tight, ba - by, you'll feel the pow er soon.
You'll beg for more, ___ you'll for - get a bout the night. ___

Chorus

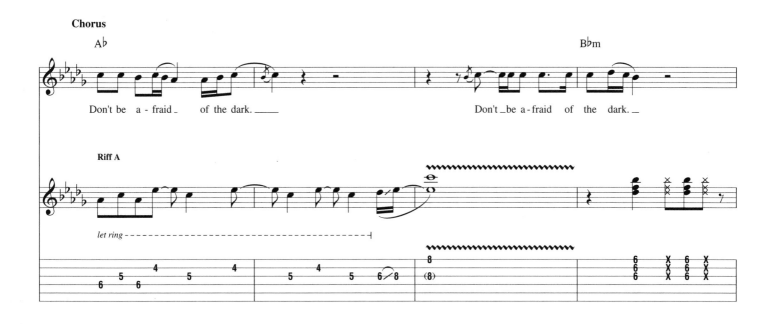

Don't be a - fraid_ of the dark.___ Don't _ be a - fraid of the dark. _

Riff A

let ring -

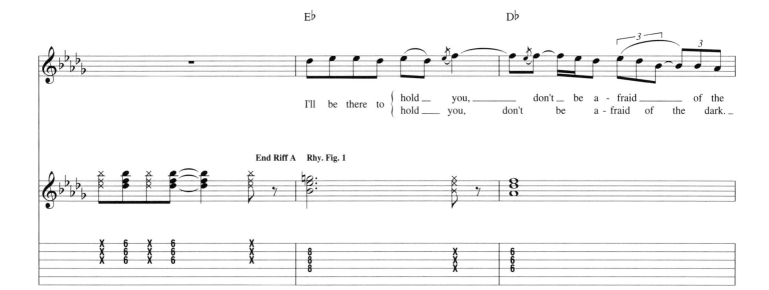

I'll be there to { hold _ you, _____ don't _ be a - fraid _____ of the
                 { hold _ you, don't be a - fraid of the dark. _

End Riff A   Rhy. Fig. 1

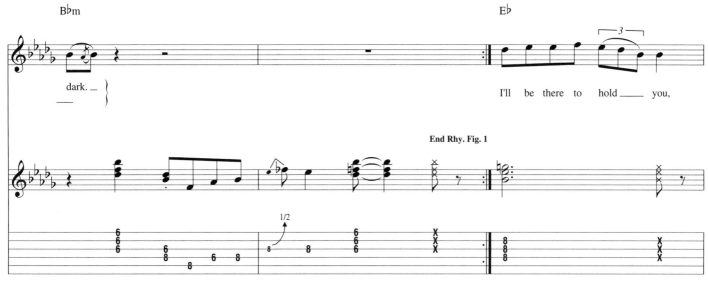

dark. _ }   I'll be there to hold ____ you,

End Rhy. Fig. 1

don't   be   a - fraid of the dark. _____

Gtr. 2 (slight dist.)

Gtr. 1

Guitar Solo

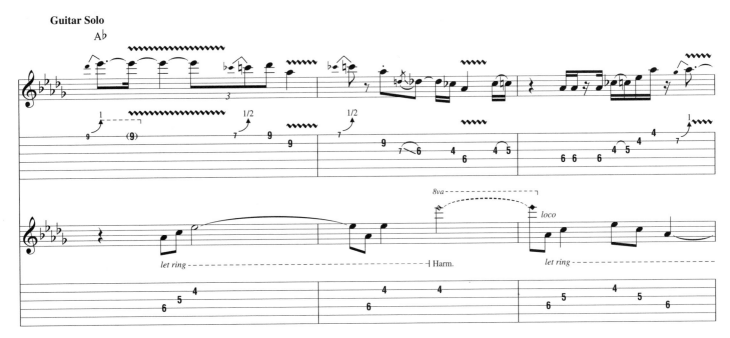

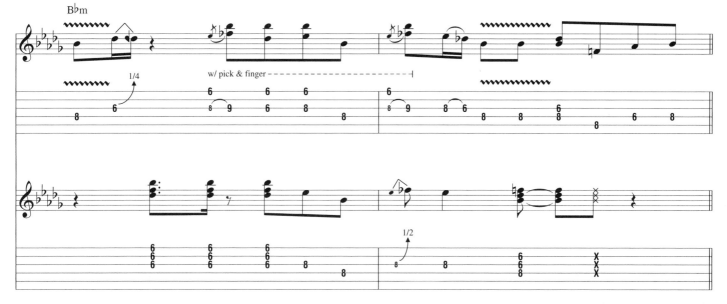

Coda

Chorus

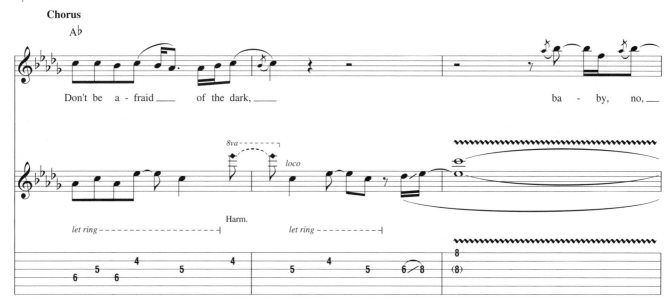

Don't be a - fraid ___ of the dark, ___ ba - by, no, ___

___ no. ___   I'll be there to hold ___ you,

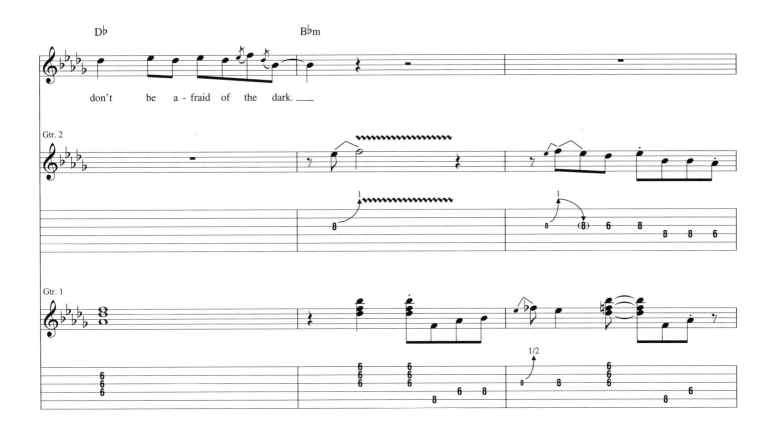

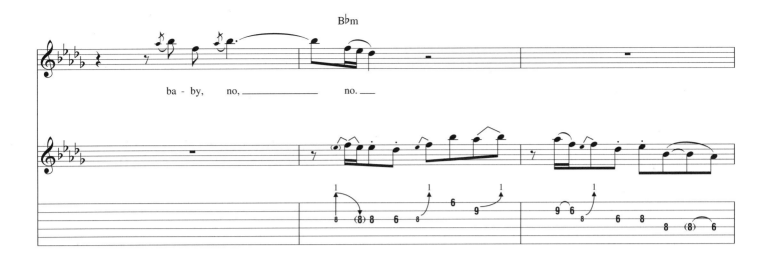

ba - by, no, _____ no. ___

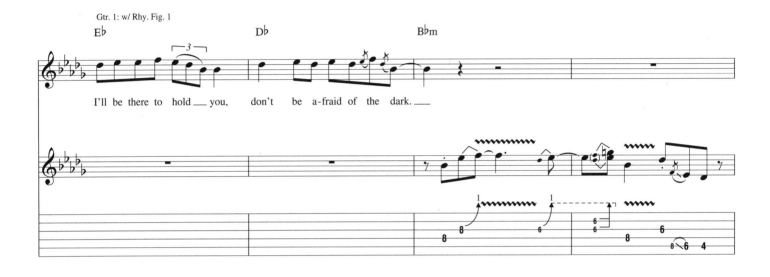

Gtr. 1: w/ Rhy. Fig. 1

I'll be there to hold __ you,   don't   be a-fraid of the dark. __

I'll be there to hold __ you,   don't   be a-fraid of the dark. _____

The Forecast (Calls for Pain)

Words and Music by David Plenn and Dennis L. Walker

Intro

*Chord symbols reflect basic harmony.

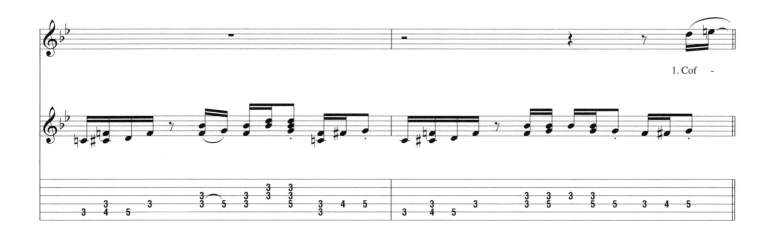

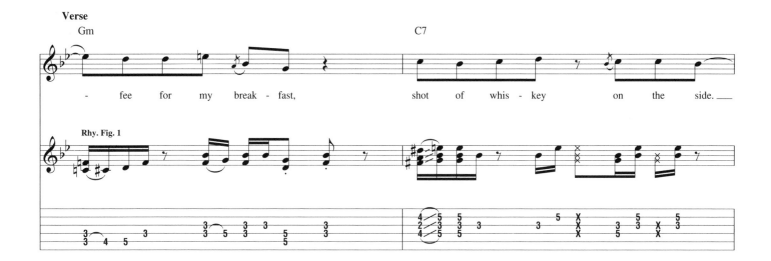

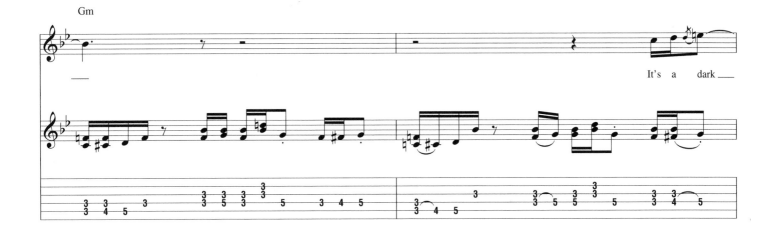

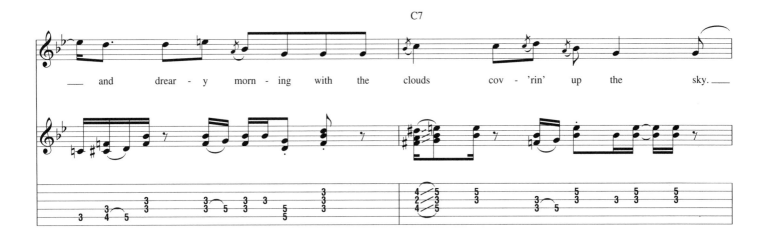

Chorus

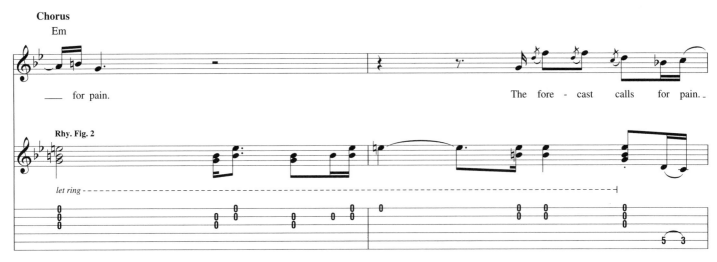

38

My ba -

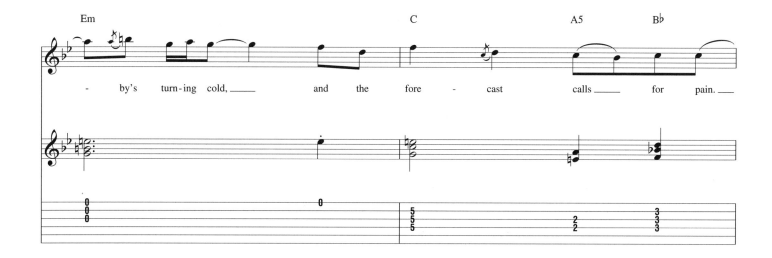

- by's turn-ing cold, _____ and the fore - cast calls _____ for pain. _____

2. We stayed

End Rhy. Fig. 2

Verse

Gtr. 1: w/ Rhy. Fig. 1

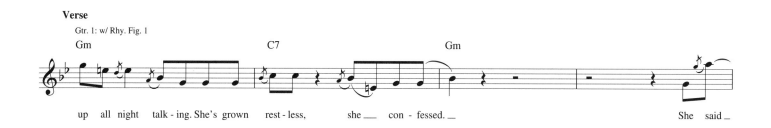

up all night talk-ing. She's grown rest-less, she _ con - fessed. _____

She said _

there's_ no one new,_ but deep down I know_ that's next._____

Chorus
Gtr. 1: w/ Rhy. Fig. 2

The fore - cast calls for pain. ____ The fore - cast calls for pain._

My ba - by's_ turn - ing cold,_ and the

fore - cast calls _ for pain. ____ She says _

Bridge

she's tried and tried,_ yes, she has,_

Gtr. 1

but slow - ly her love has died. I can see _

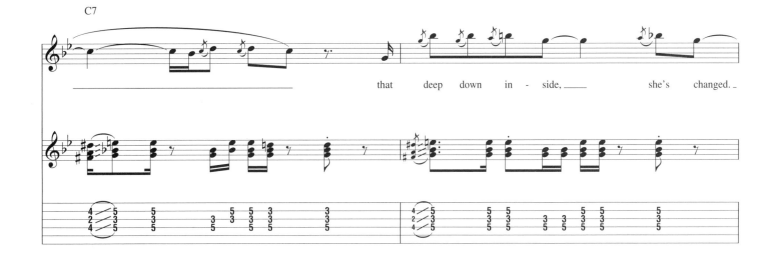

that deep down in - side, ____ she's changed. ____

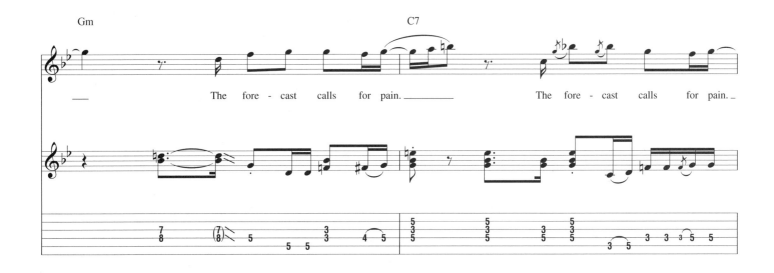

____ The fore - cast calls for pain. ____ The fore - cast calls for pain. ____

____ Fore - cast calls for pain, _____ yeah, _____ yeah, ____

Gtr. 2 (clean)

8va -

f

w/ slap-back delay

Gtr. 1

Guitar Solo

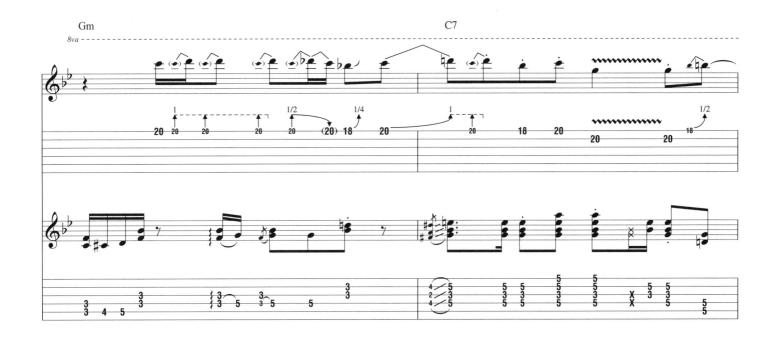

3. I can hear ___

Verse

Gtr. 1: w/ Rhy. Fig. 1   Gtr. 2 tacet

Gm   C7   Gm

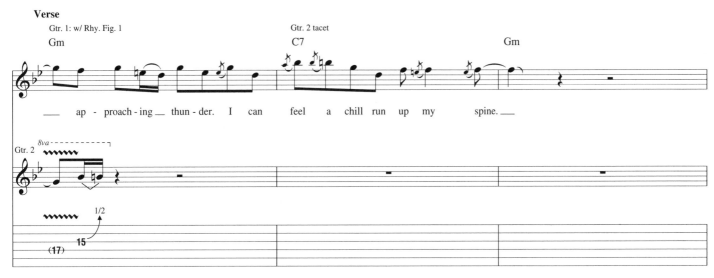

___ ap - proach - ing ___ thun - der. I can   feel   a   chill   run up   my   spine. ___

Gtr. 2

-ning.   Yeah!   I   feel   the   pain.

Riff A   End Riff A

Gtr. 1: w/ Riff A (till Fade)

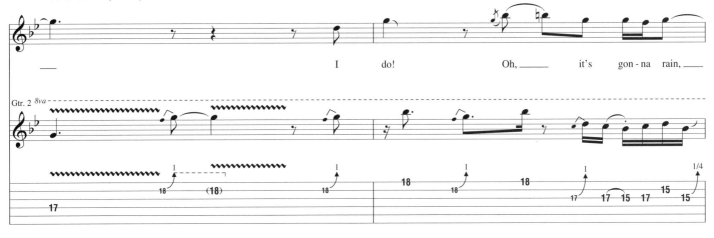

               I   do!   Oh,   it's   gon - na   rain,

Gtr. 2 8va

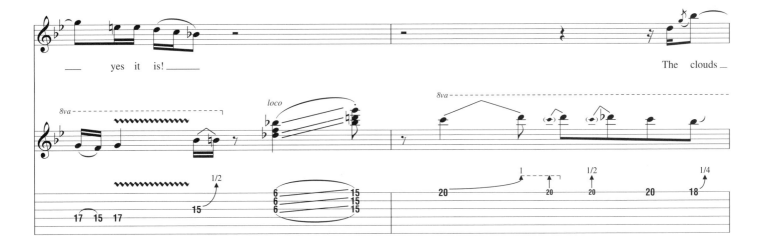

     yes it is!   The   clouds

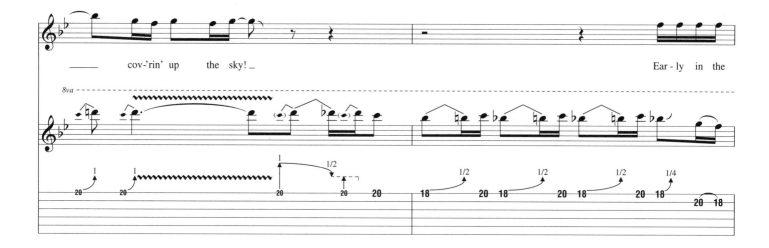

_____ cov-'rin' up the sky! _____ Ear-ly in the

Begin fade

morn - ing. _____ Yeah! All day, all day. In the morn - ing, uh! Yeah! _____

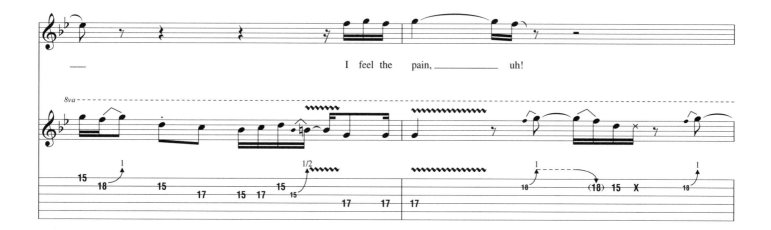

_____ I feel the pain, _____ uh!

Fade out

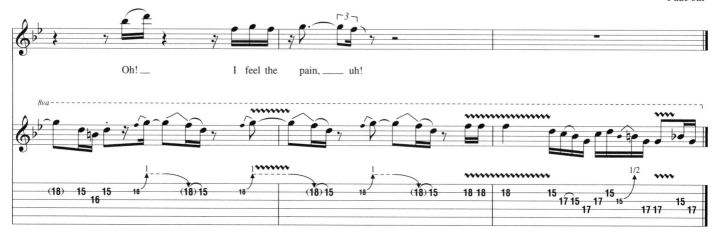

Oh! _____ I feel the pain, _____ uh!

from *Strong Persuader*

Nothin' but a Woman

Words and Music by Bruce M. Bromberg, Robert Cray, Peter Boe, Richard Cousins and David Olson

Intro
Moderately fast ♩ = 131

*C7

Gtr. 1 (clean)

mf

let ring throughout

P.M.

*Chord symbols reflect basic harmony.

Riff A

End Riff A

**Gtr. 2

mf

**Horn section arr. for gtr.

Gtr. 1

Gtr. 2: w/ Riff A

1. You can

Gtr. 1

Verse

give me an hour ___ a - lone in a bank, ___ pay all my tick - ets, wipe the slate blank. ___ You could
fly us to Dal - las on a jum - bo jet plane. _ If we run late and miss it, we can take the night train. ___ When the

Riff B

2nd time, Gtr. 1: w/ Fill 1

buy me a car, ___ fill up the tank, _ tell me a boat full of law - yers just sank. ___ But it ain't
pres - sure is on, ___ things get - ting in - sane, _ there's on - ly one cure for that ___ kind of strain. _ It

End Riff B

Chorus

2nd time, Gtr. 1: w/ Fill 1

noth - in' but a wom - an, _ noth - in' but a wom - an, no, _ no. ___ Don't need

Riff C

Fill 1
Gtr. 1

noth- in' but a { wom- an
          wom- an, yeah, _____

an -y - time _____ I'm feel - ing low. _____
get   me through the _____ show. _

2. Well, you can

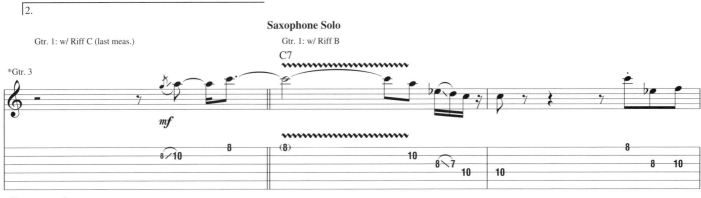

2.

Saxophone Solo

Gtr. 1: w/ Riff C (last meas.)   Gtr. 1: w/ Riff B

*Gtr. 3

*Tenor sax arr. for gtr.

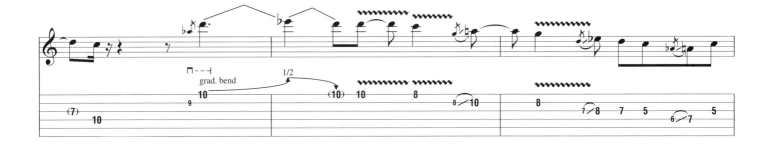

grad. bend   1/2

Gtr. 1: w/ Riff C

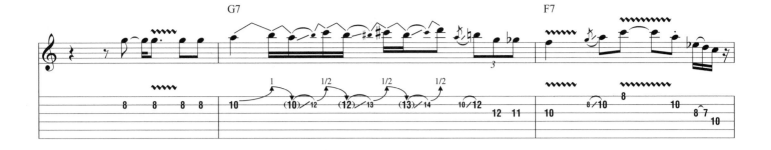

Guitar Solo

Gtr. 1: w/ Riff B (1st 7 meas.)
Gtr. 3 tacet

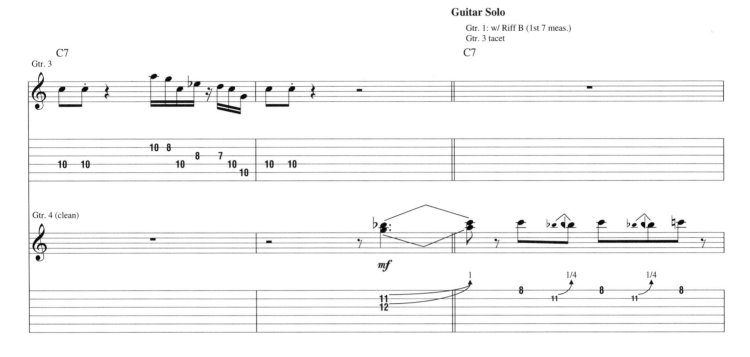

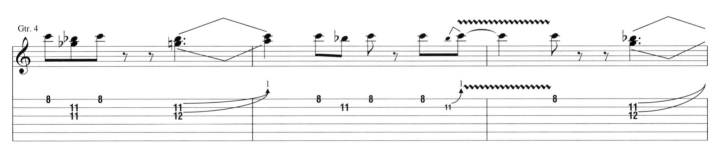

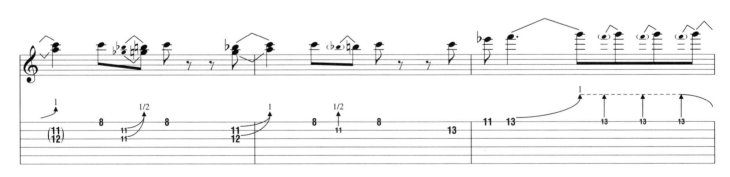

Gtr. 1: w/ Fill 1

Gtr. 1: w/ Riff C

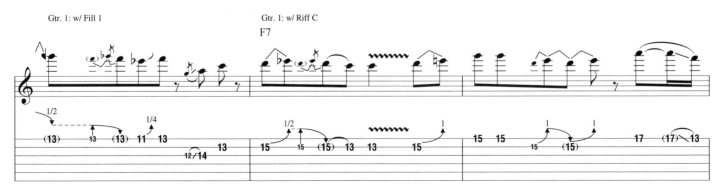

Nothing Against You

Words and Music by Robert Cray

2nd time, Gtr. 1: w/ Rhy. Fill 1
3rd time, Gtr. 1: w/ Rhy. Fill 2

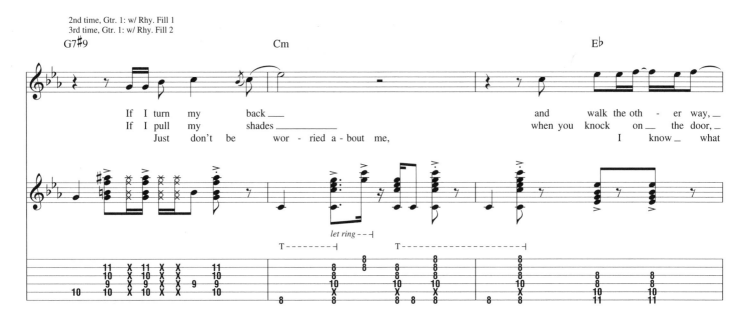

If I turn my back ___ and walk the oth - er way, ___
If I pull my shades ___ when you knock on the door,
Just don't be wor - ried a - bout me, I know ___ what

3rd time, Gtr. 1: w/ Rhy. Fill 3

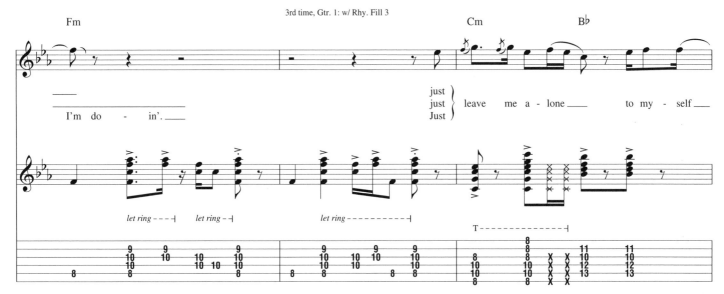

___
___ I'm do - in'. ___

just
just } leave me a - lone ___ to my - self ___
Just

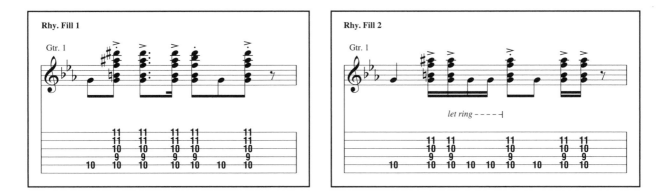

Rhy. Fill 1

Rhy. Fill 2

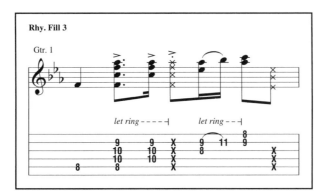

Rhy. Fill 3

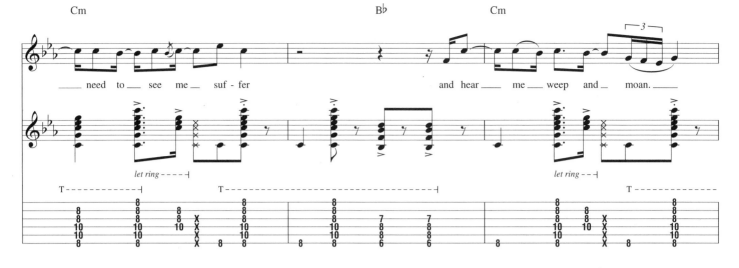

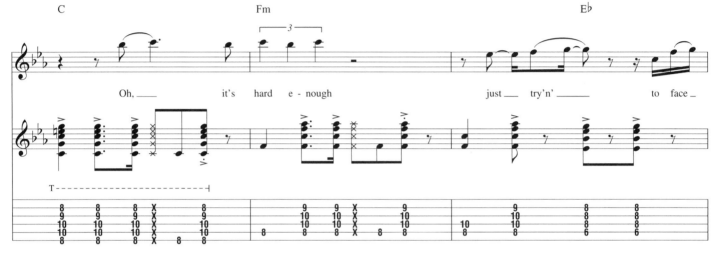

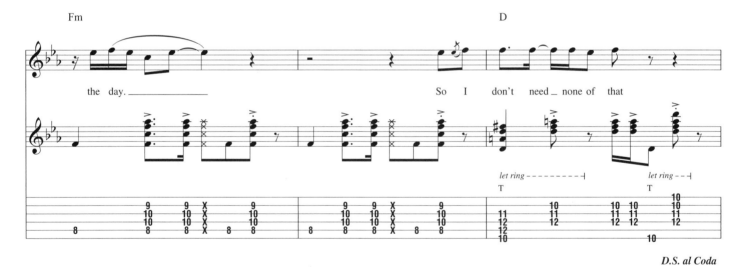

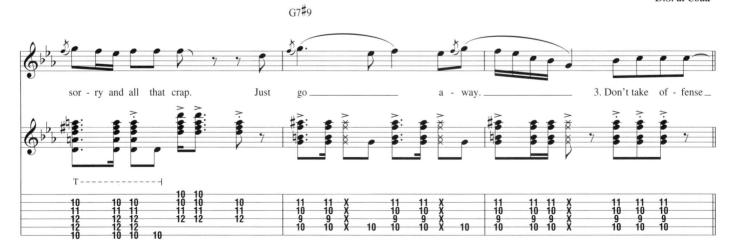

Coda

Outro-Guitar Solo

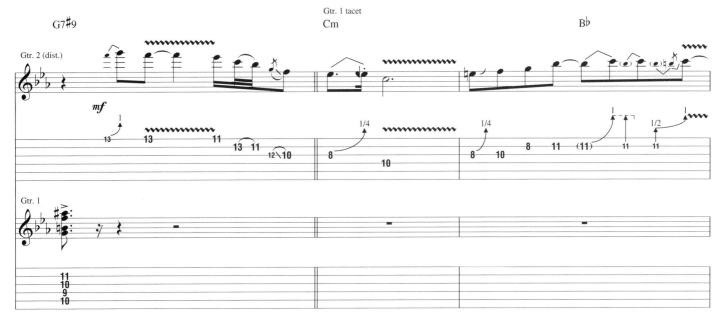

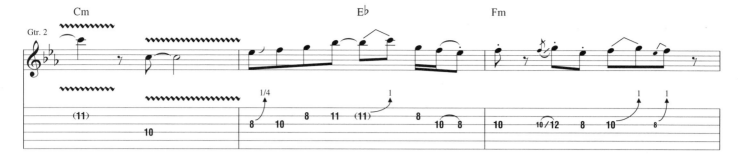

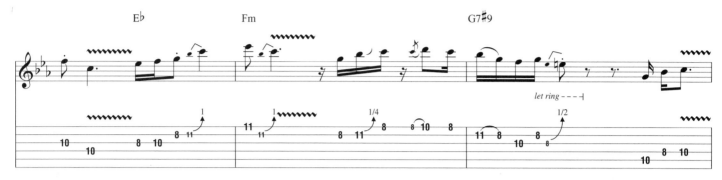

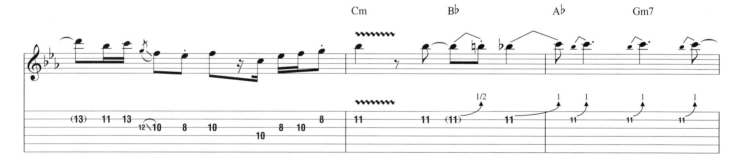

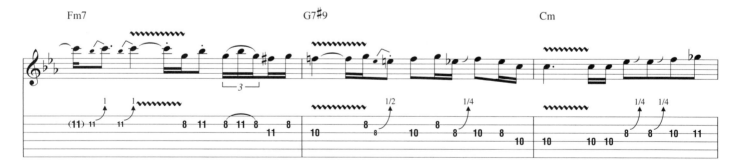

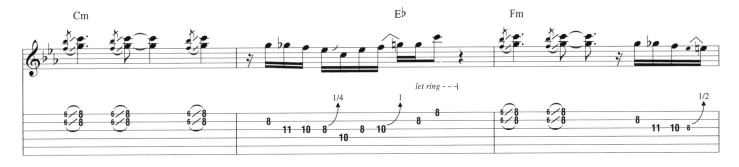

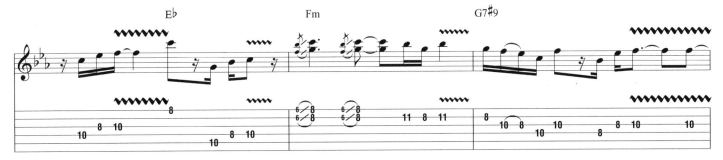

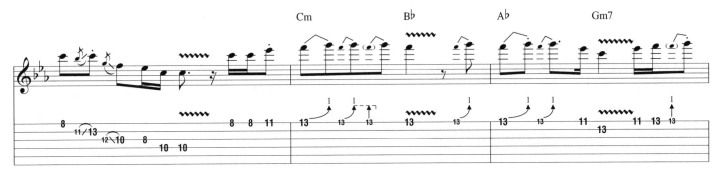

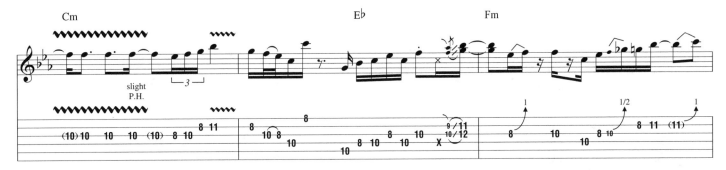

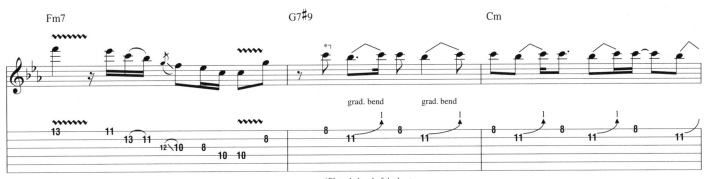

*Played ahead of the beat.

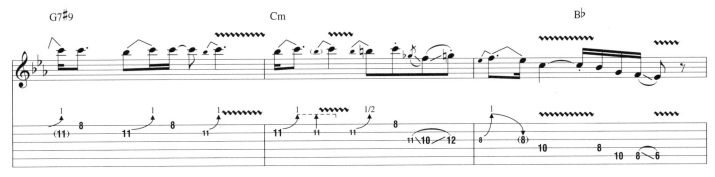

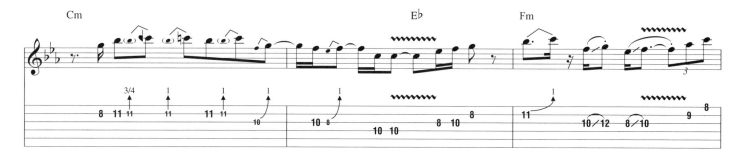

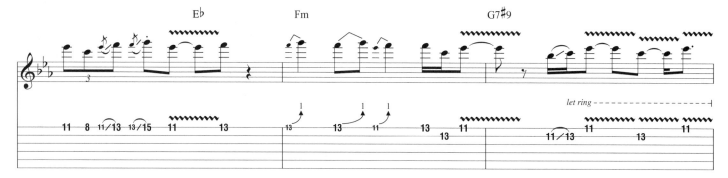

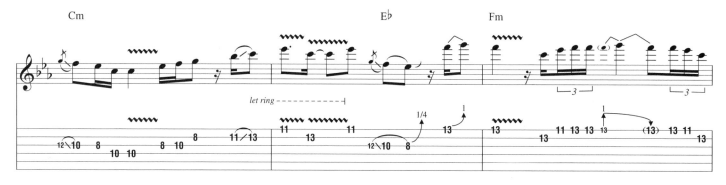

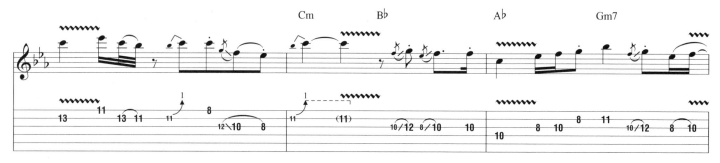

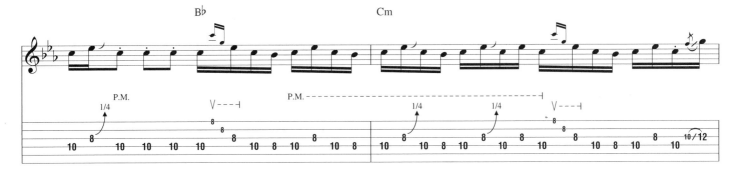

Begin fade

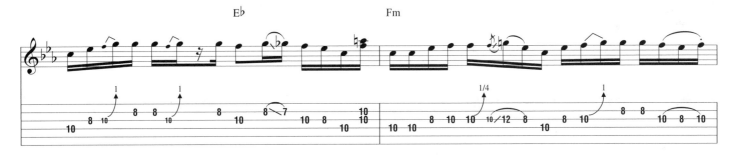

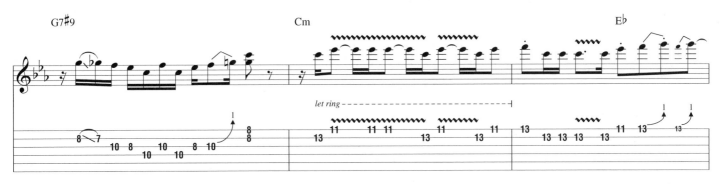

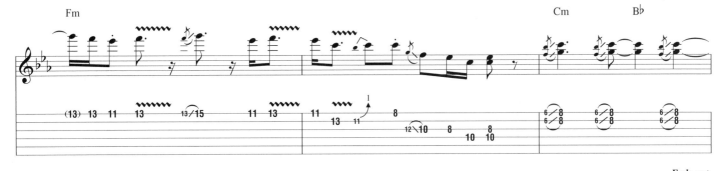

Fade out

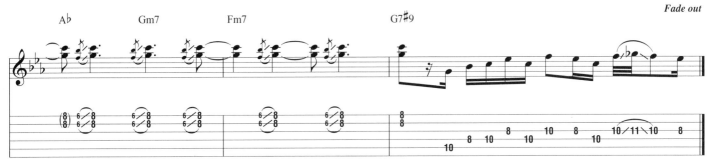

from *Bad Influence*

Phone Booth

Words and Music by Robert Cray, Richard Cousins, Michael Vannice and Dennis L. Walker

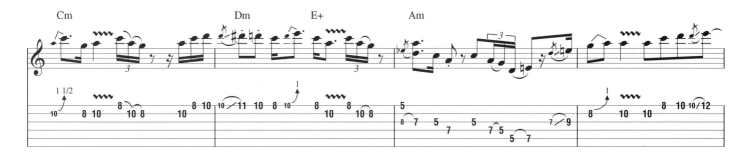

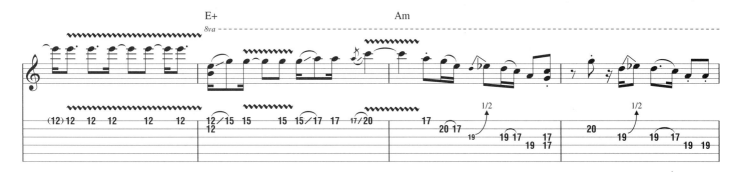

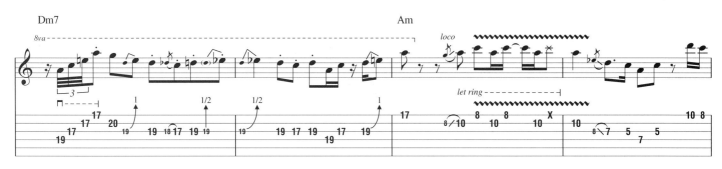

D.S. al Coda
(take repeat)

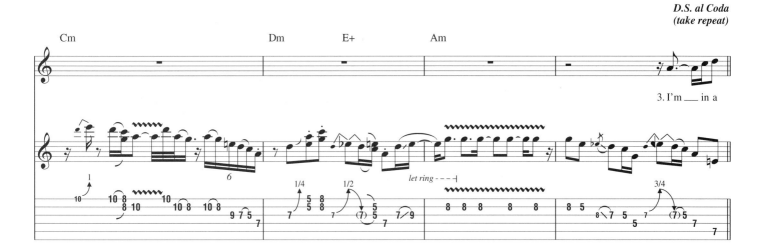

3. I'm ___ in a

⊕ Coda

Outro-Guitar Solo

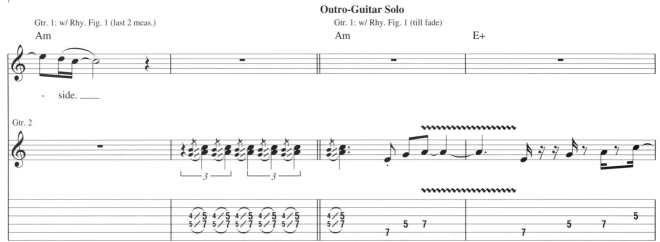

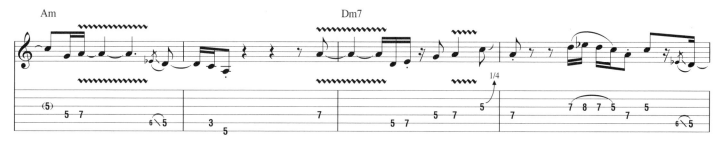

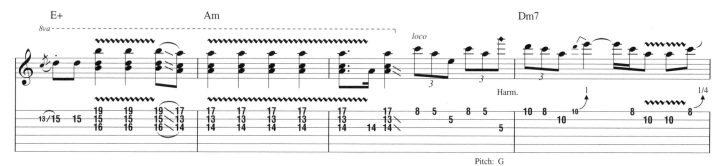

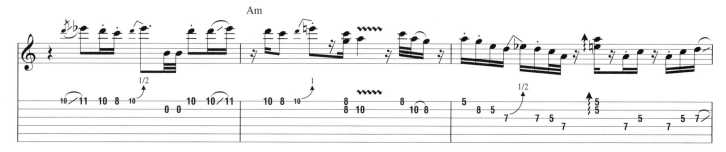

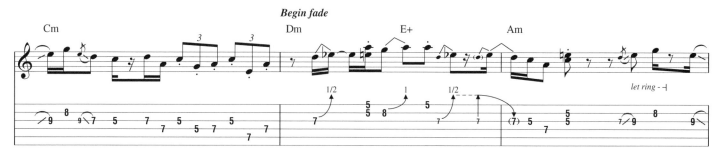

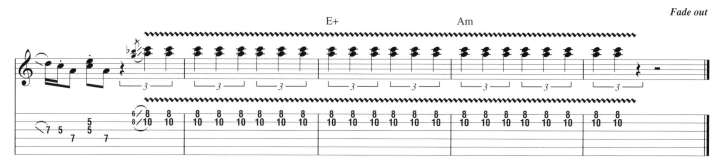

65

Playin' with My Friends

Words and Music by Dennis L. Walker and Robert Cray

and a few of the la-dies I know.___   I'm gon-na___

End Riff A

Gtr. 3: w/ Riff A

___ rent a hall ___ and   get them all ___ and   put on a ___ heck of a show.___

Gtr. 1

Gtr. 2

Make sure we got a kitch - en, with a ov - en and a stove. We'll all get in there

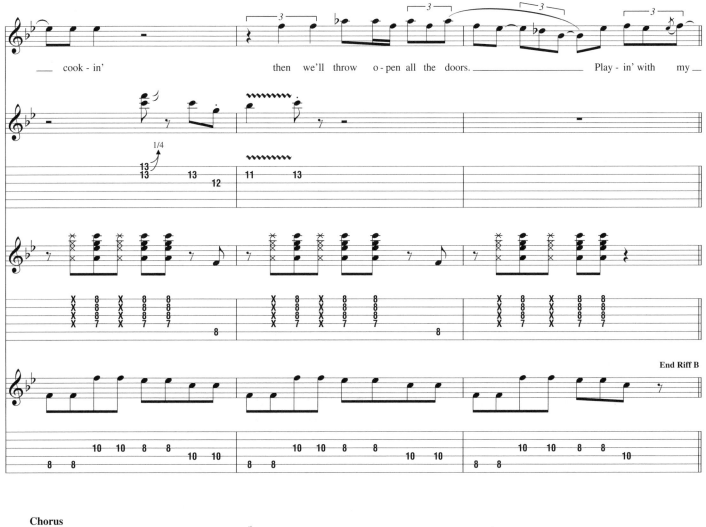

___ cook - in'   then we'll throw o - pen all the doors. ___ Play - in' with my ___

End Riff B

Chorus

C7   F7#9   Bb7

___ friends.   Play - in' with my ___ friends.

- fish,   cook it all up on the grill. ___

Bake __ some beans ___ and corn - bread,   ev - 'ry - bod - y's gon - na get their __

fle,   and man, _____ we'll have a ball.   Play - in' with my

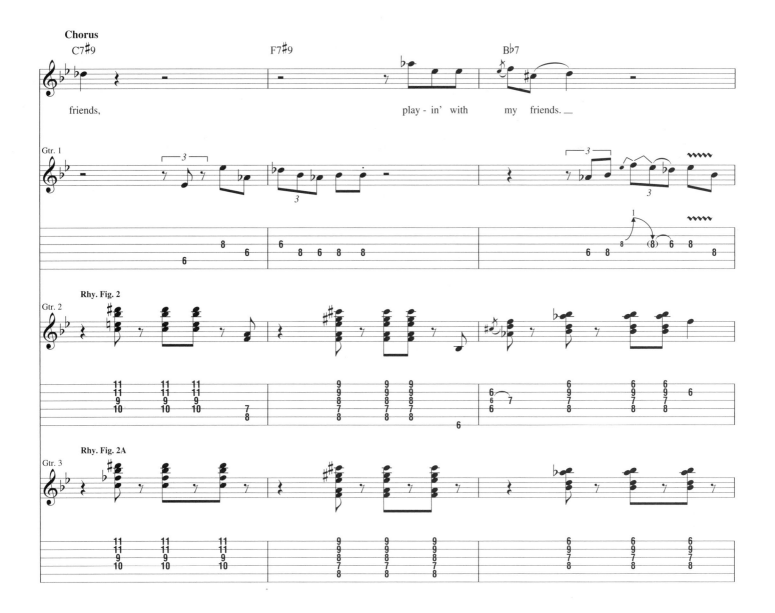

friends,   play - in' with   my   friends. __

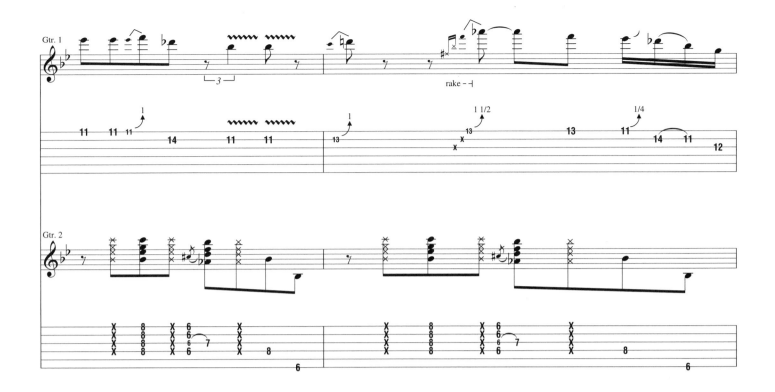

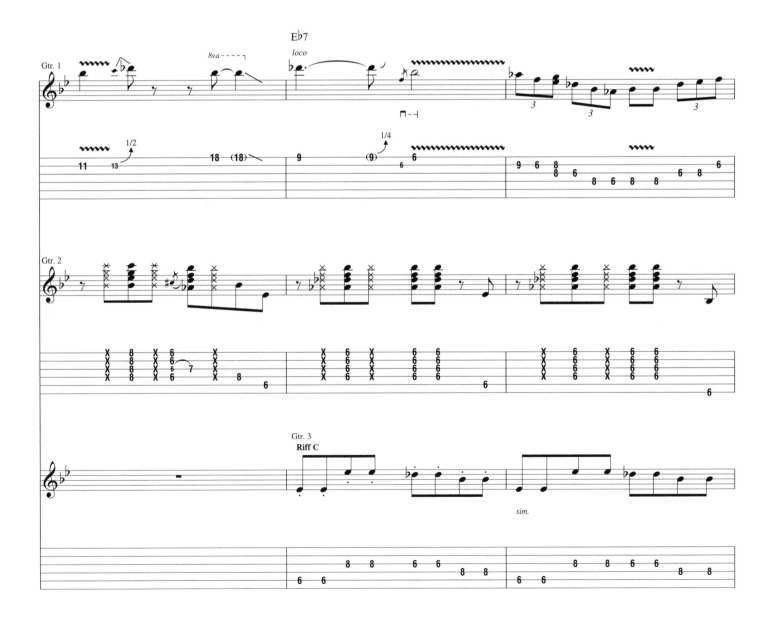

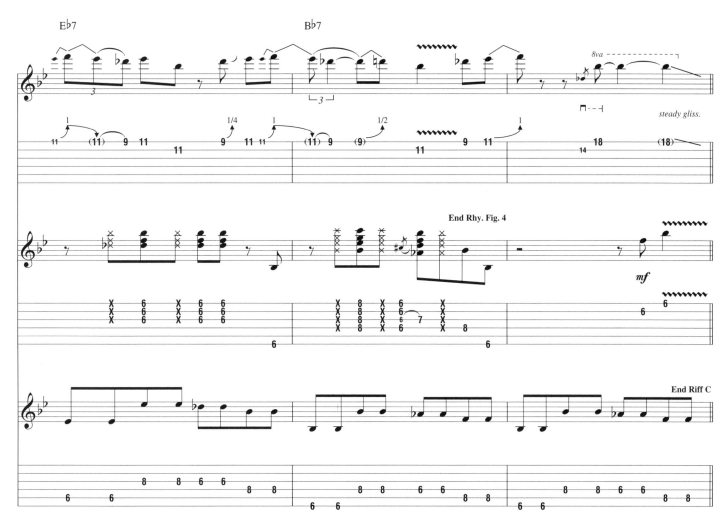

Guitar Solo

Gtr. 1 tacet
Gtr. 3 w/ Riff A

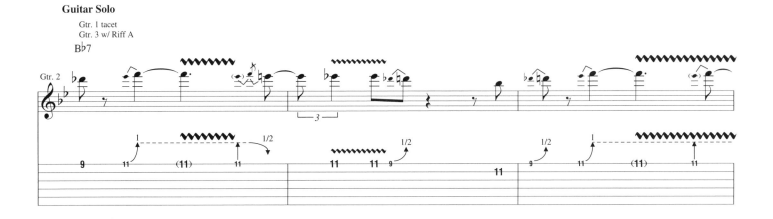

Gtr. 3: w/ Riff C

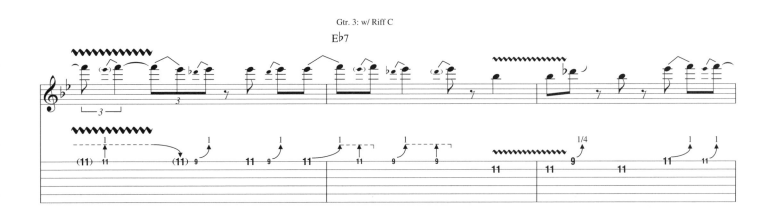

Robert Cray: 3. Yes, _____ we're gon - na

Verse

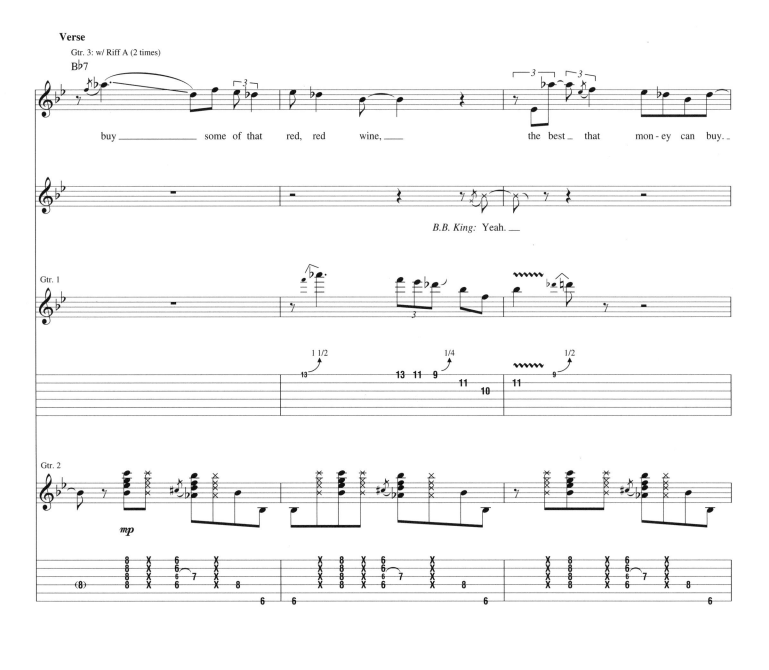

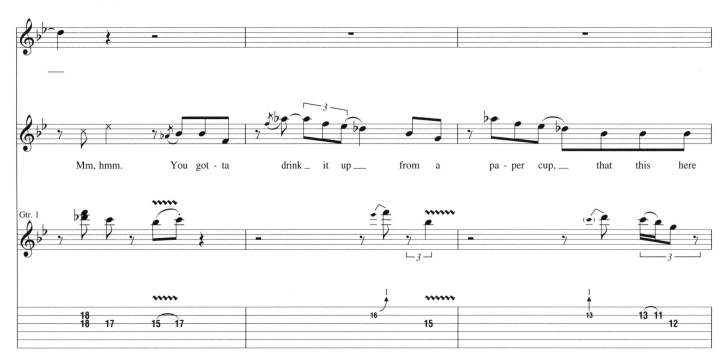

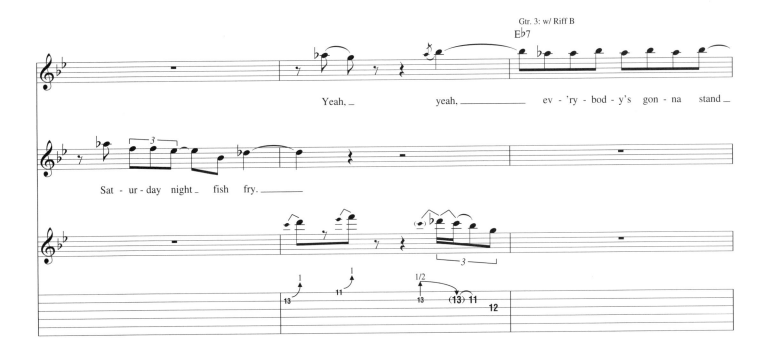

Yeah, __ yeah, _____ ev - 'ry - bod - y's gon - na stand _

Sat - ur - day night _ fish fry. _____

__ up, play _____ their fa - vor - ite tune.

Yeah. Mm, __ hmm. You can

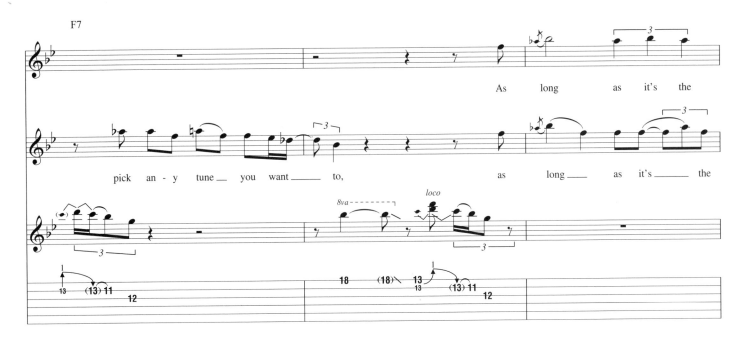

As long as it's the

pick an - y tune _ you want _____ to, as long ____ as it's _____ the

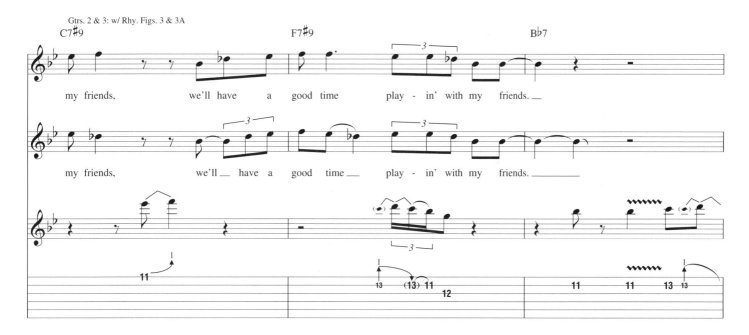

my friends,   we'll have a   good time   play - in' with my   friends. ___

my friends,   we'll ___ have a   good time ___ play - in' with my   friends. ___

Guitar Solo

Gtr. 2: w/ Rhy. Fig. 4
Gtr. 3: w/ Riff A

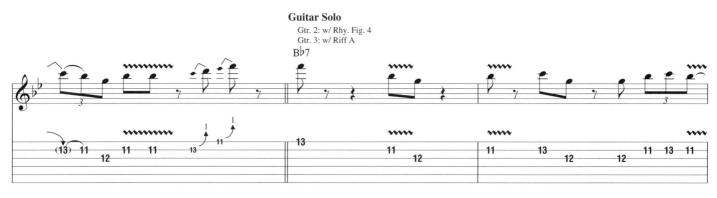

Gtr. 3: w/ Riff C

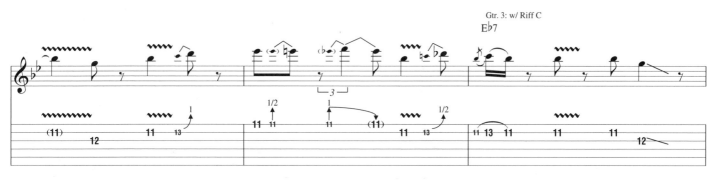

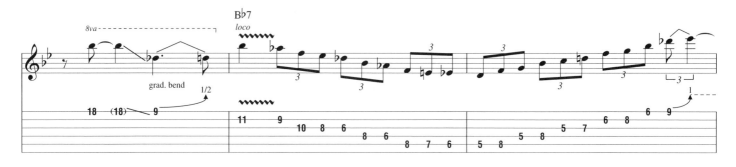

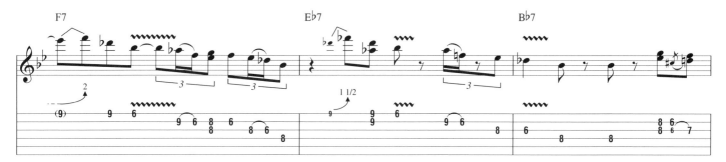

Guitar Solo

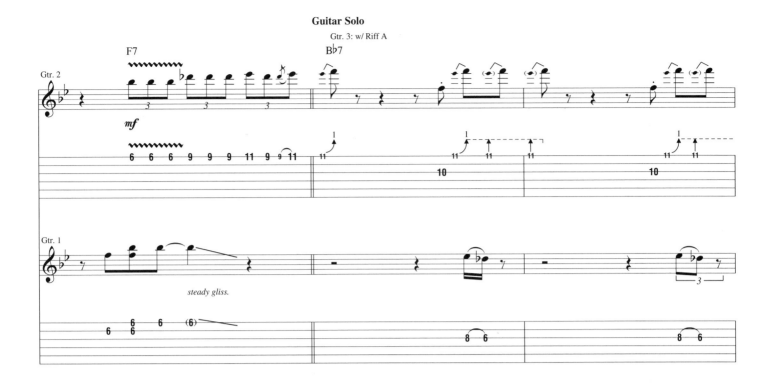

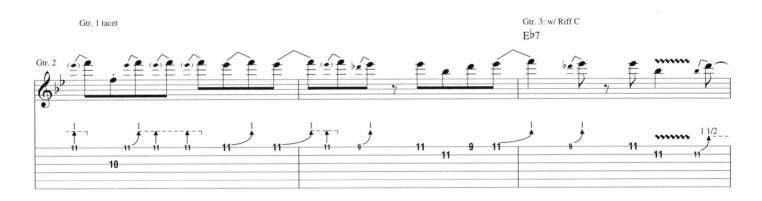

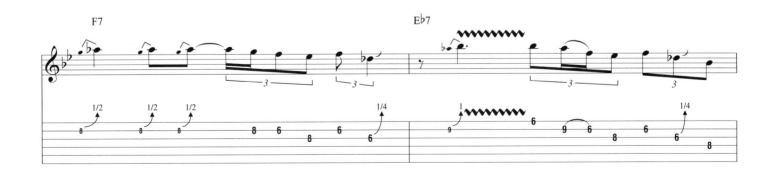

Guitar Solo

Gtr. 2: w/ Rhy. Fig. 4
Gtr. 3: w/ Riff A

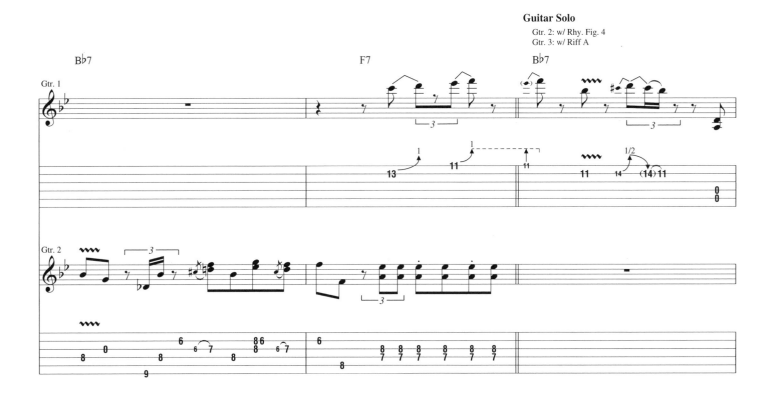

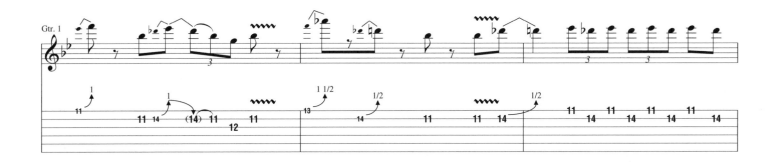

Gtr. 3: w/ Riff C

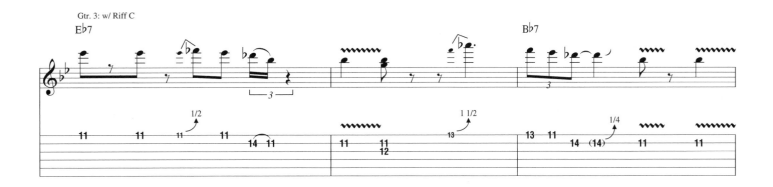

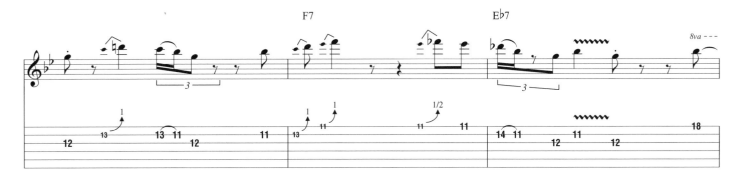

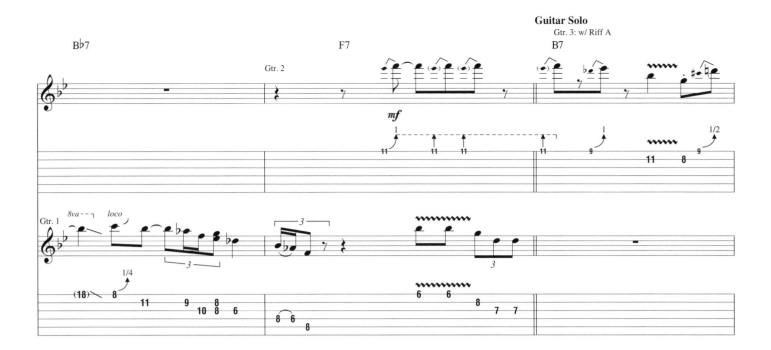

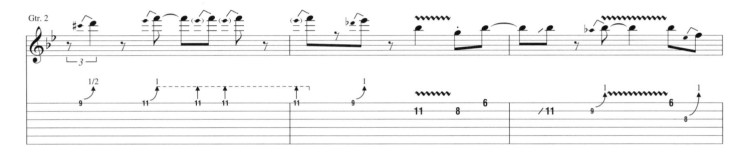

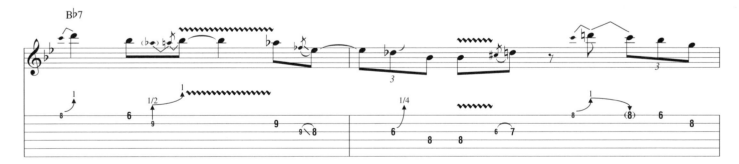

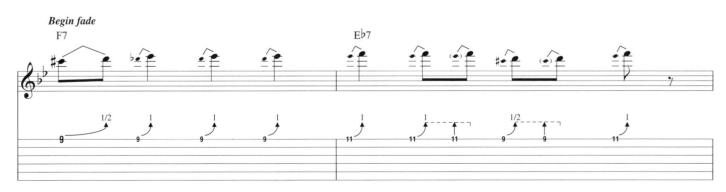

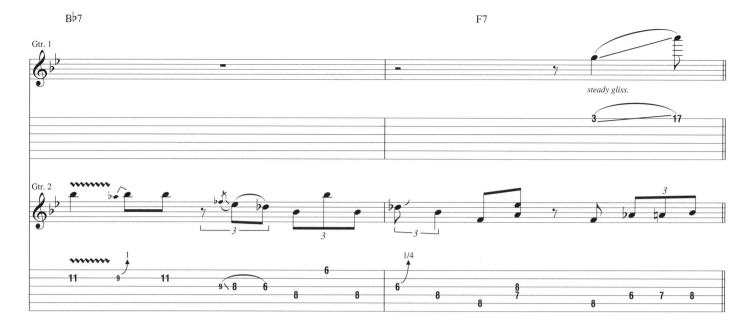

Outro-Guitar Solo

Gtr. 3: w/ Riff A

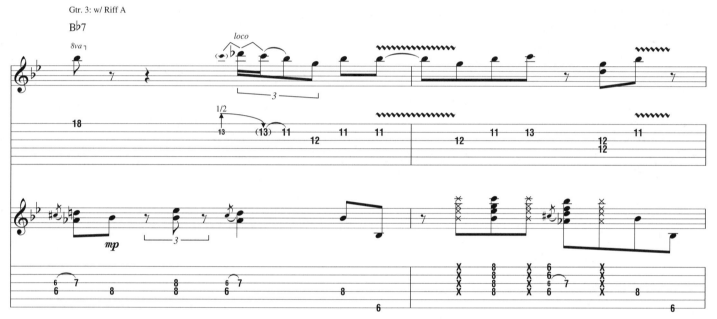

Gtr. 2: w/ Rhy. Fig. 4 (meas. 3-8)

Gtr. 3: w/ Riff C (till fade)

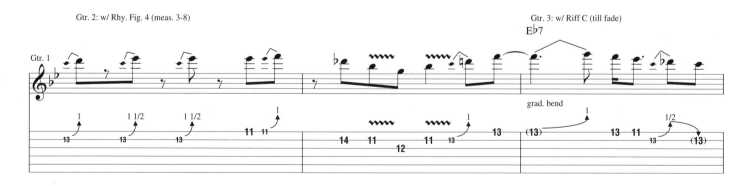

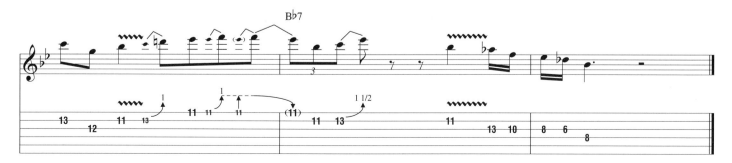

from *Twenty*

Poor Johnny

Words and Music by Robert Cray

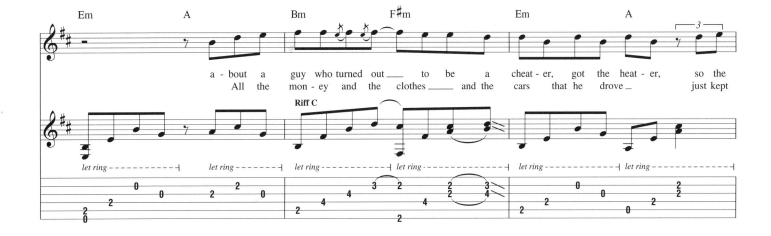

a - bout a guy who turned out____ to be a cheat - er, got the heat - er, so the
All the mon - ey and the clothes____ and the cars that he drove____ just kept

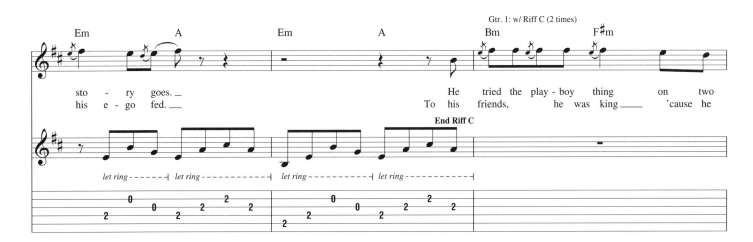

sto - ry goes. ____
his e - go fed. ____

He tried the play - boy thing on two
To his friends, he was king____ 'cause he

friends, think - in' that they'd nev - er know. ____
thought of ev - 'ry-thing ex - cept his num - ber one. ____

They say he got caught in a
She had the kids and the house while

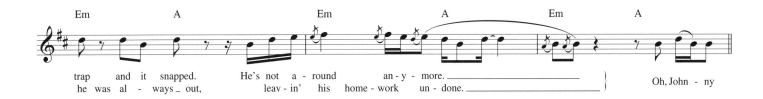

trap and it snapped. He's not a - round an - y - more. ____
he was al - ways __ out, leav - in' his home - work un - done. ____

Oh, John - ny

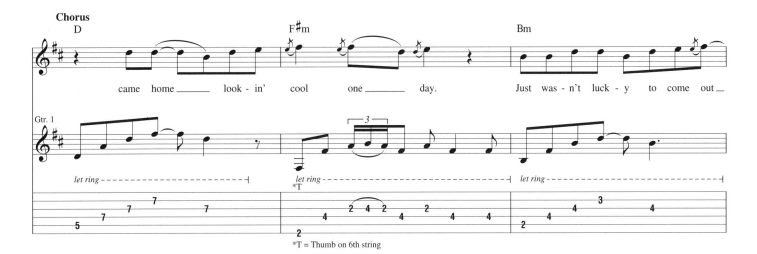

came home ____ look - in' cool one ____ day.
Just was - n't luck - y to come out ____

*T = Thumb on 6th string

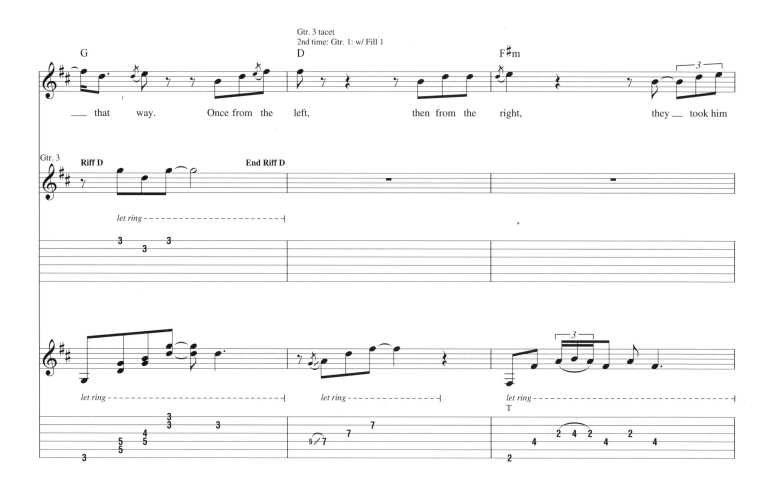

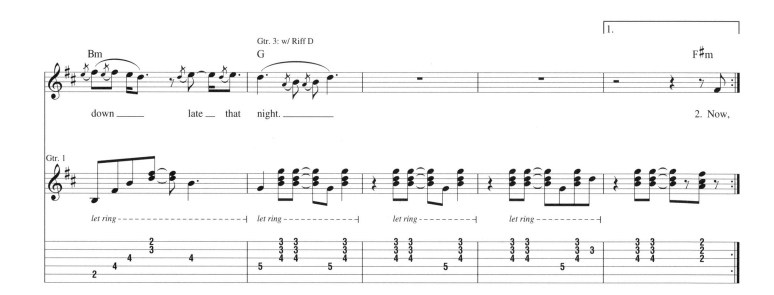

*Fender Rhodes arr. for gtr.

talked all night, they had to _____ teach him a les - son, they had to make things _ right. _

Guitar Solo

Gtr. 1: w/ Riff C (4 times)
Gtrs. 3 & 4 tacet
Gtr. 5 (slight dist.)

*w/ delay

*Set for half-note regeneration w/ 1 repeat.

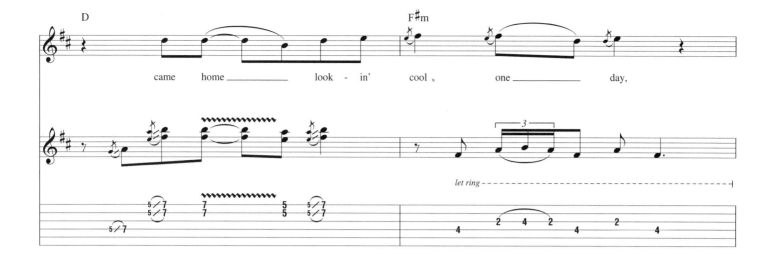

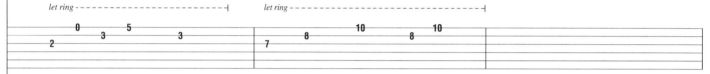

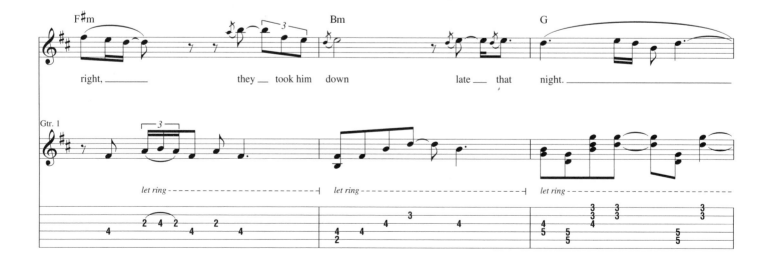

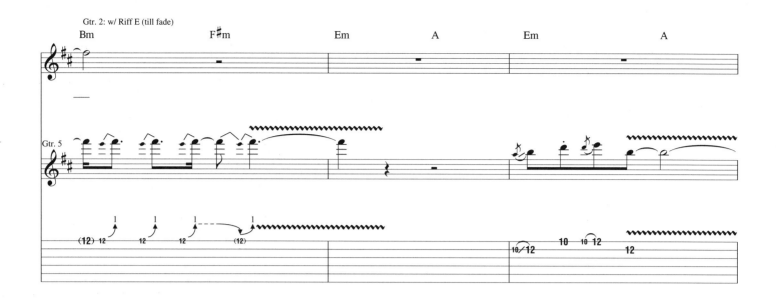

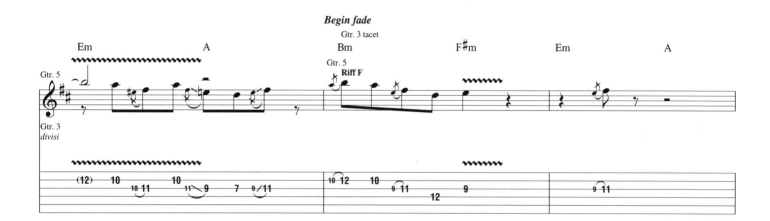

Right Next Door

By Dennis Walker

Intro

Moderately slow ♩ = 92

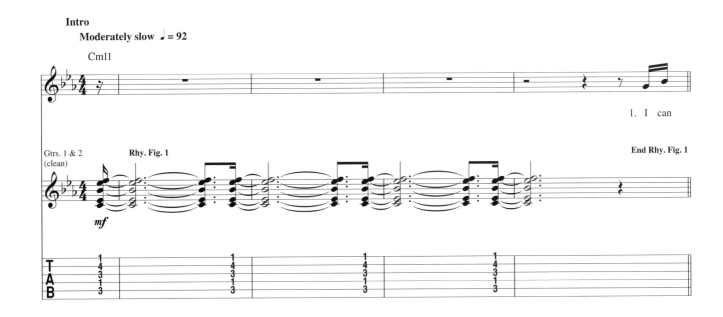

1. I can

Verse

hear the cou - ple fight - in' ___ right ___ next door; ___ their an - gry

*Chord symbols reflect overall harmony.

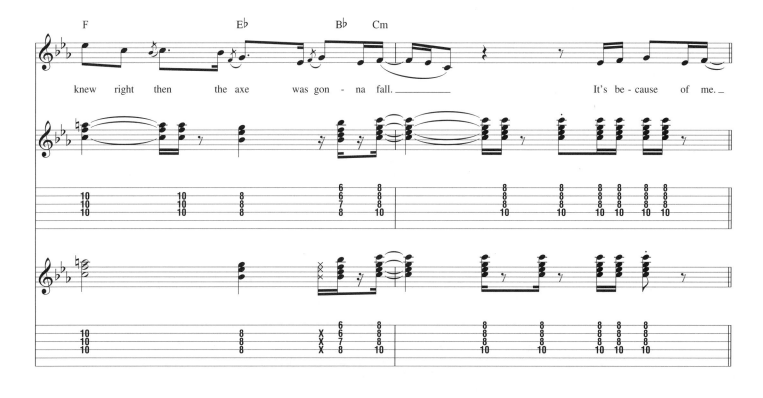

knew right then the axe was gon - na fall._____ It's be - cause of me._

Pre-Chorus

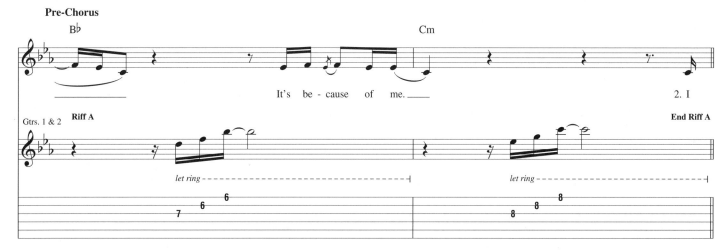

It's be - cause of me._____ 2. I

Verse

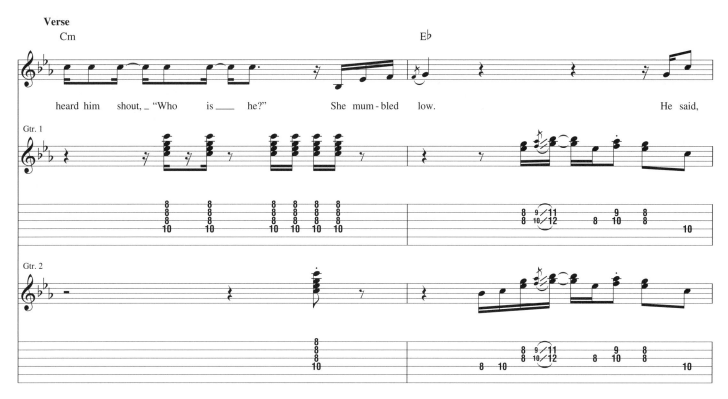

heard him shout, _ "Who is ____ he?" She mum - bled low. He said,

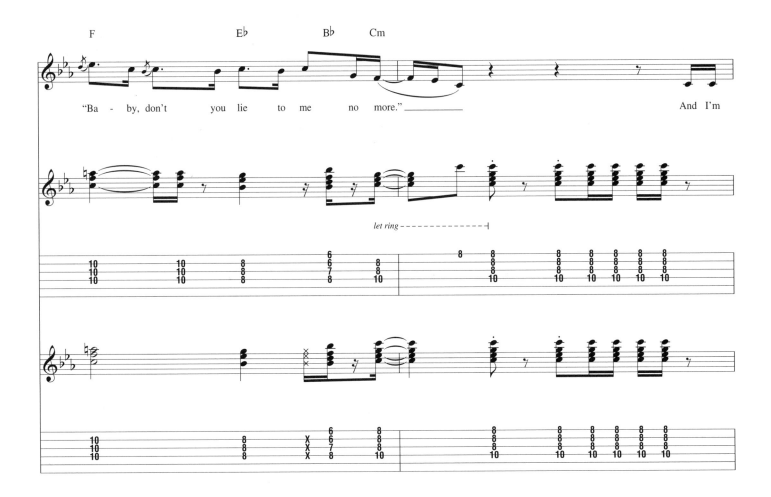

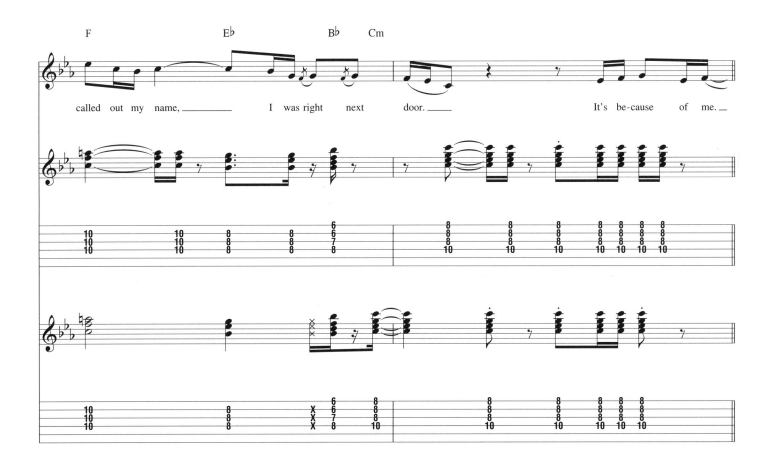

called out my name,_____ I was right next door._____ It's be-cause of me.__

Pre-Chorus

Gtr. 2: w/ Riff A (2 times)

It's be-cause of me.____ Be-cause _

Gtr. 1

let ring -----------------------

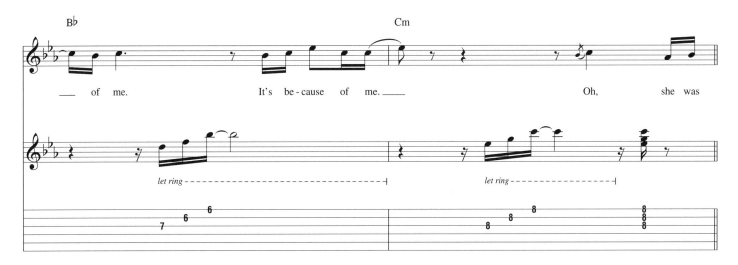

__ of me. It's be-cause of me.____ Oh, she was

let ring -----------------------

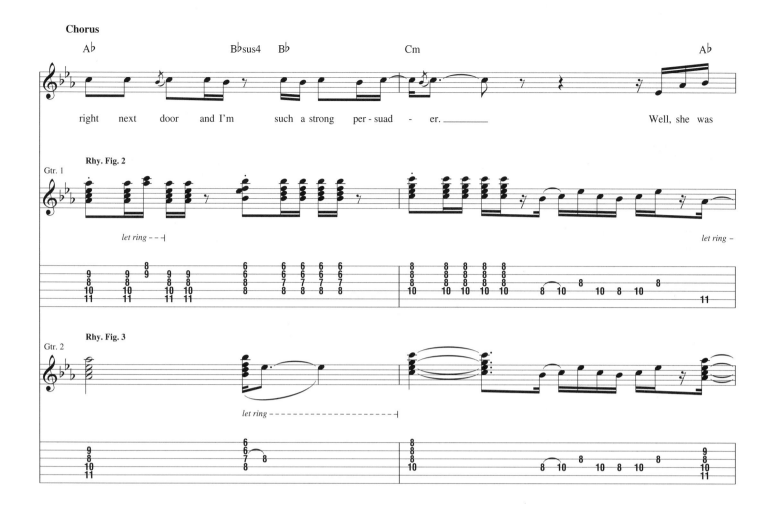

right next door and I'm such a strong per-suad - er._____ Well, she was

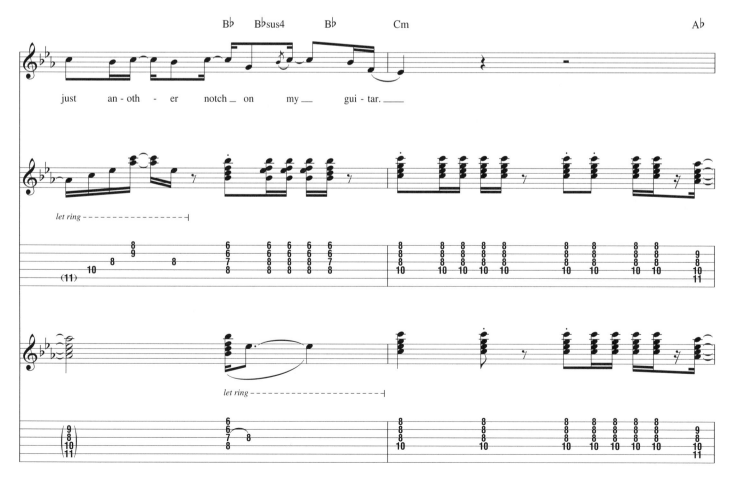

just an-oth - er notch_ on my _ gui-tar.____

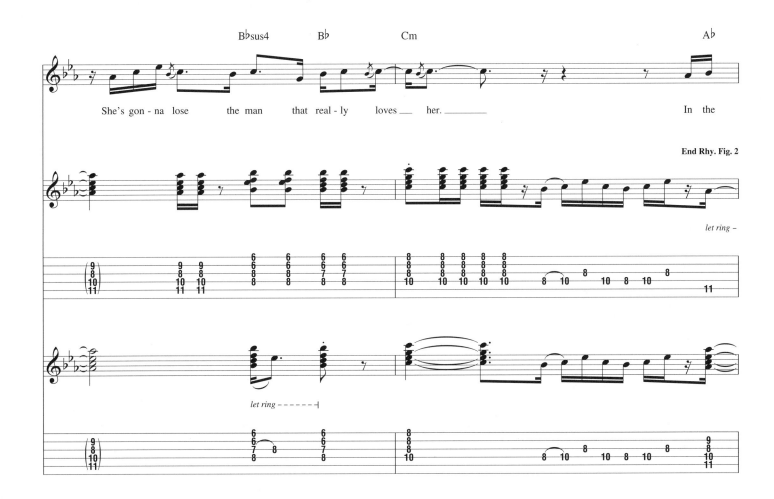

She's gon-na lose the man that real-ly loves her. In the

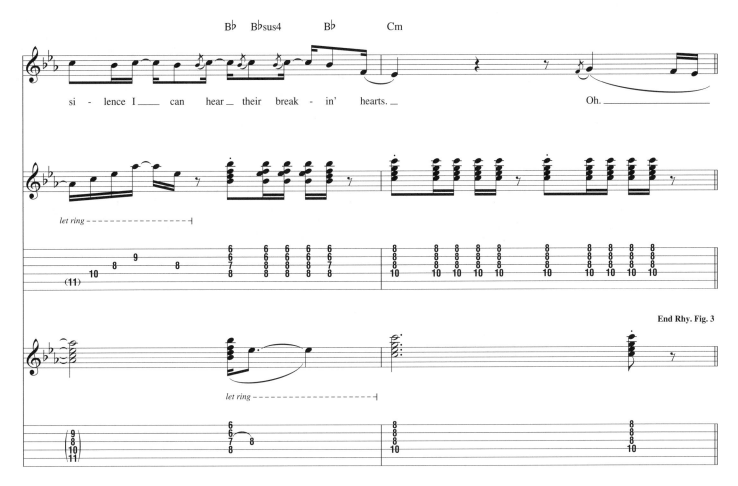

si-lence I can hear their break-in' hearts. Oh.

Interlude

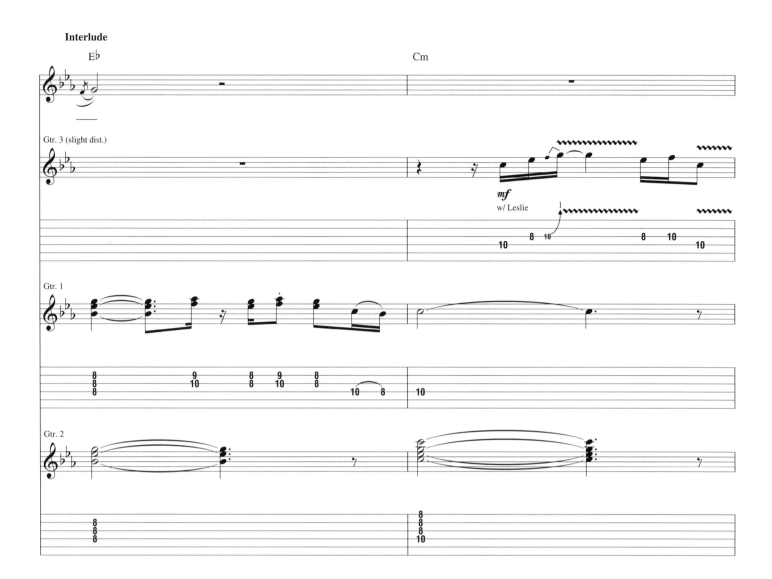

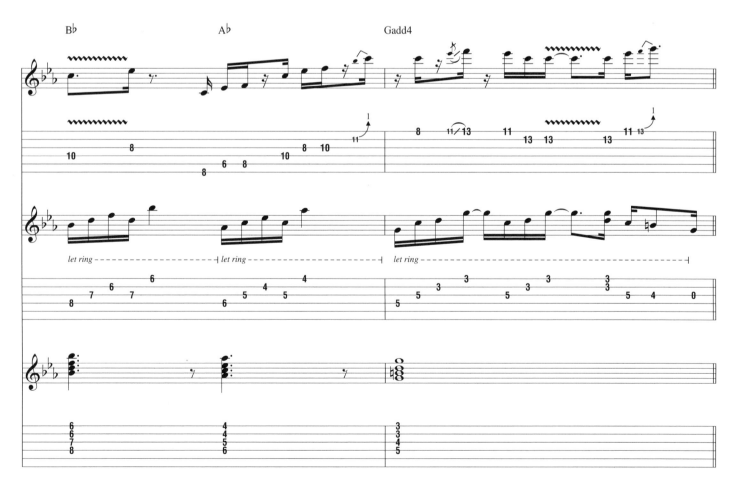

Guitar Solo

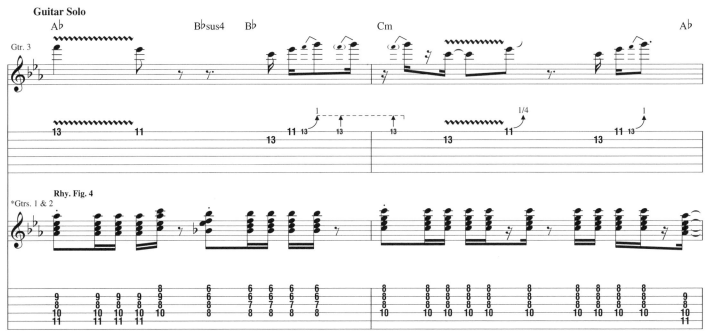

*Composite arrangement

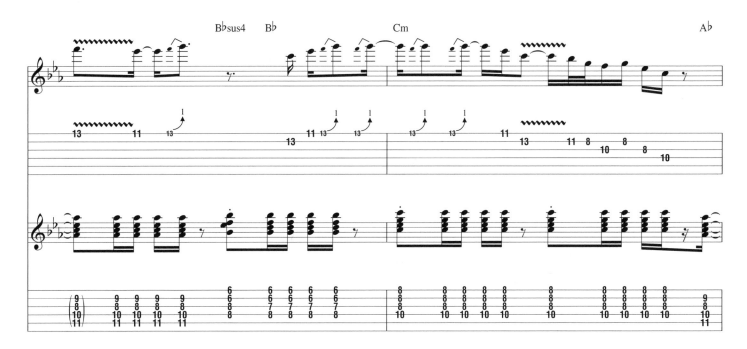

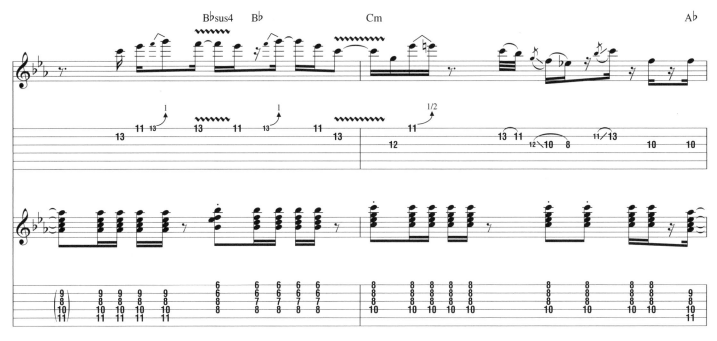

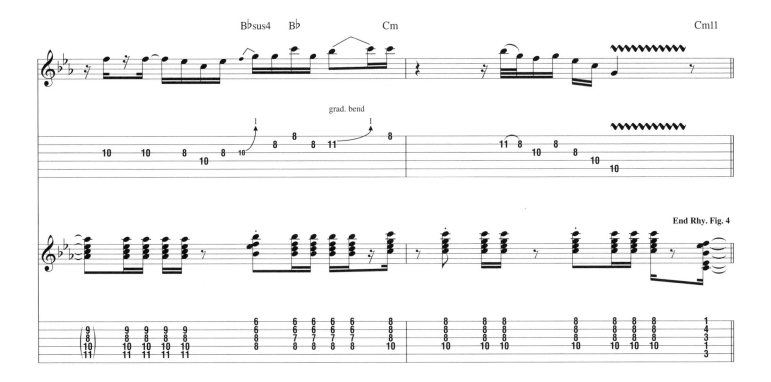

End Rhy. Fig. 4

Interlude

Gtrs. 1 & 2: w/ Rhy. Fig. 1

Cm11

Gtr. 3

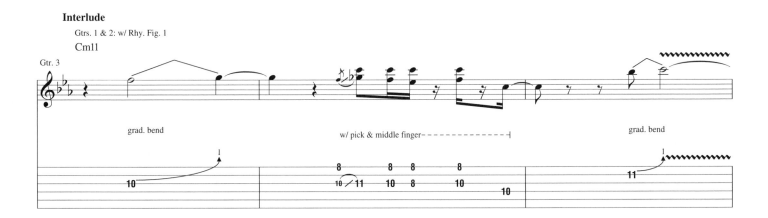

grad. bend

w/ pick & middle finger- - - - - - - - - - - - - - - -

grad. bend

Verse

Gtr. 3 tacet

Cm

3. At day-break I hear him pack, ___ say good-

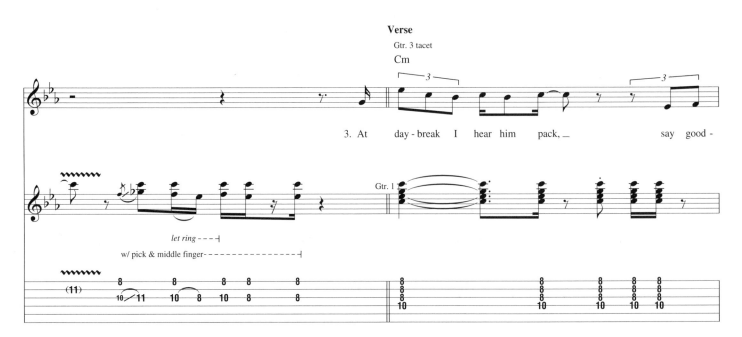

let ring - - - -

w/ pick & middle finger- - - - - - - - - - - - - - - - -

Gtr. 1

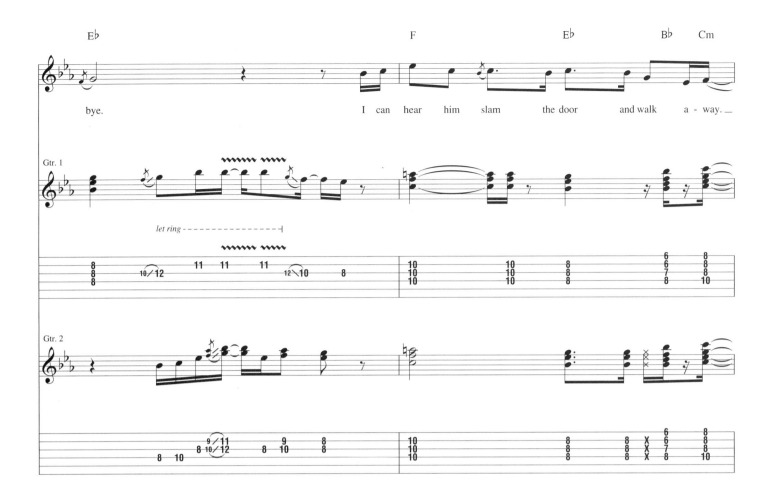

bye.   I can hear him slam   the door   and walk   a - way.

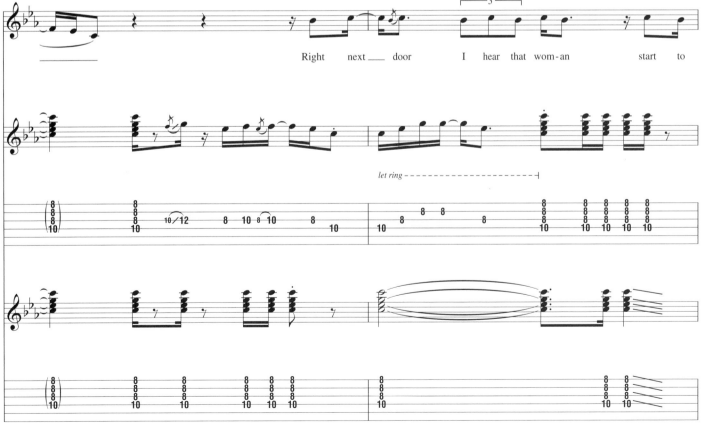

Right next ___ door   I hear that wom-an   start to

*Sung behind
the beat.

105

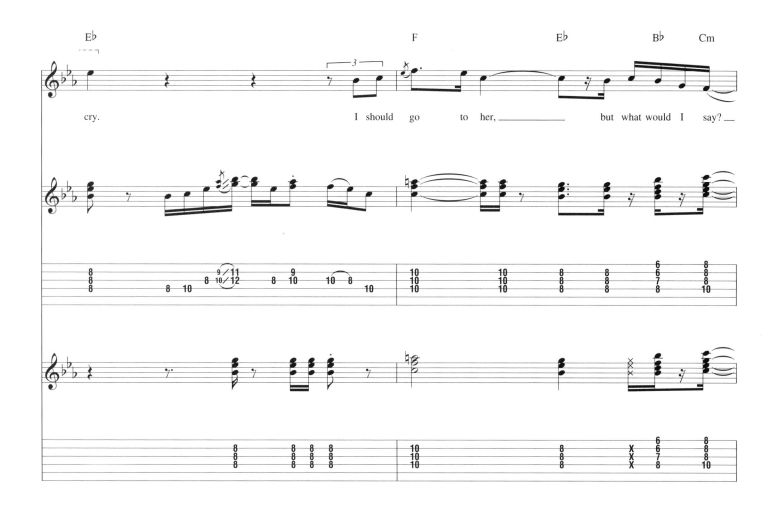

cry.   I should go to her, _____ but what would I say? ___

Pre-Chorus

Gtr. 2: w/ Riff A (2 times)

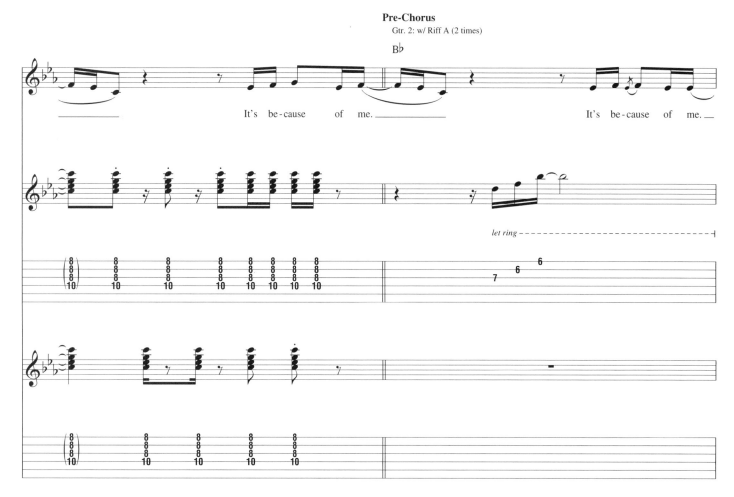

_____ It's be-cause of me. _____ It's be-cause of me. ___

let ring -

Chorus
Gtr. 1: w/ Rhy. Fig. 2

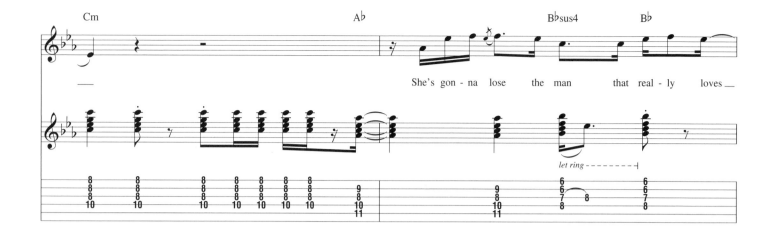

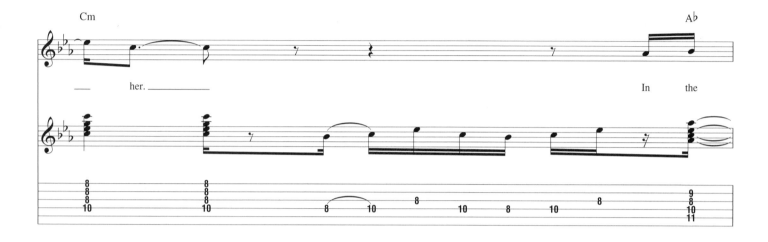

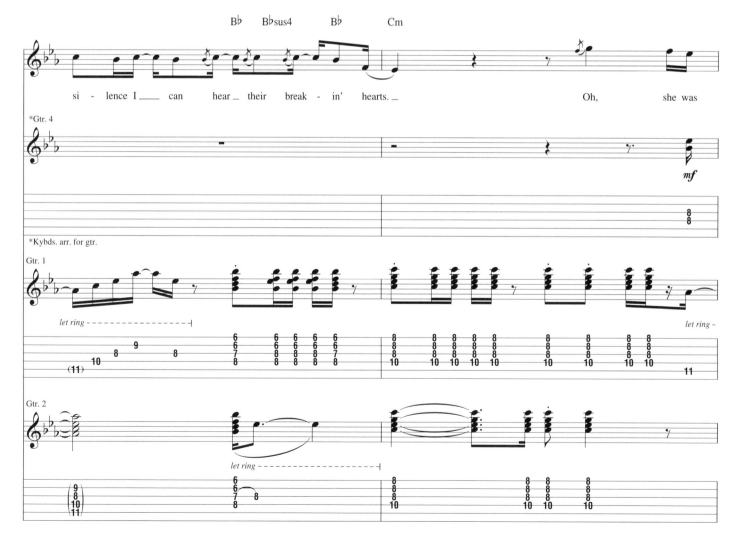

right next door and I'm such a strong per - suad - er, _____ yeah. ____

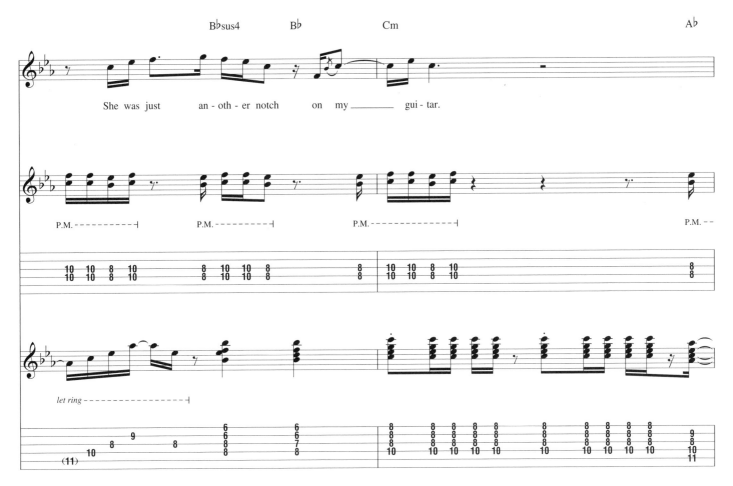

She was just an - oth - er notch on my _____ gui - tar.

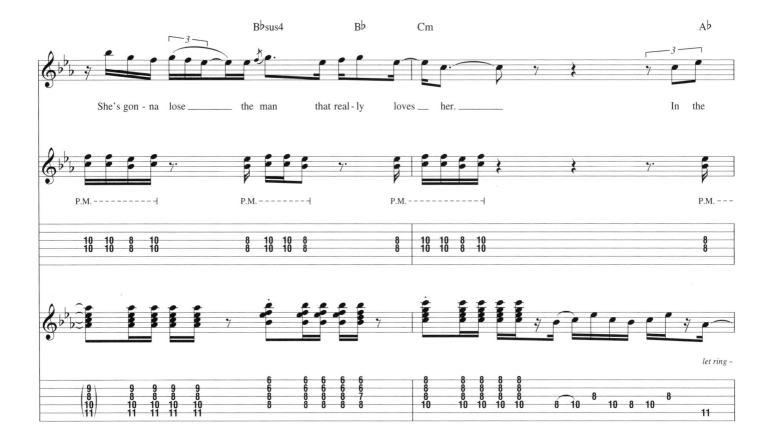

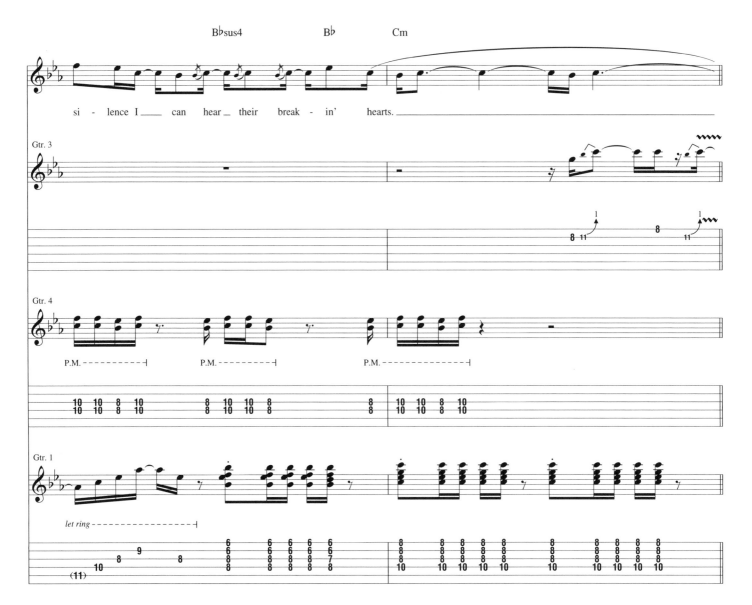

Guitar Solo

Gtrs. 1 & 2: w/ Rhy. Fig. 4
Gtr. 4 tacet

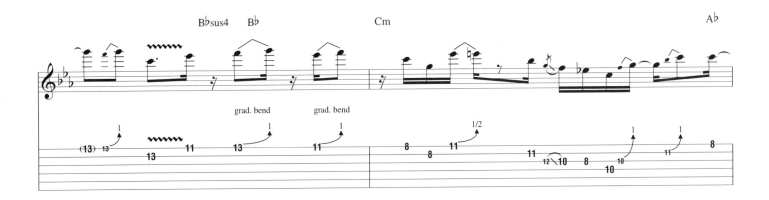

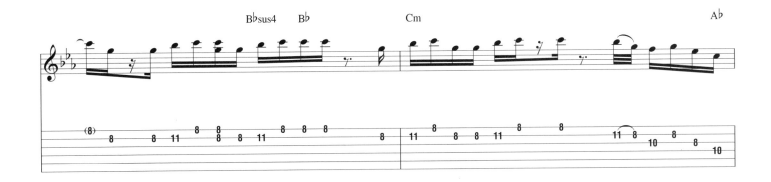

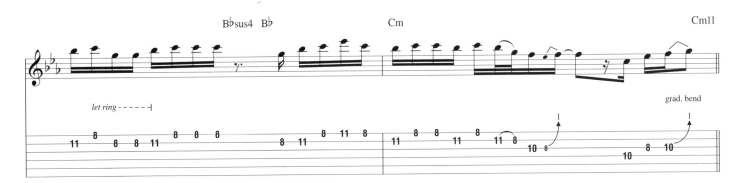

Outro

Gtrs. 1 & 2: w/ Rhy. Fig. 1 (1st 2 meas., 4 times)

Cm11

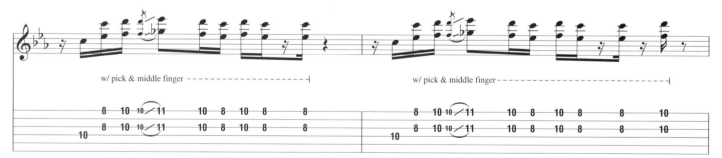

Begin fade

Fade out

She's Into Somethin'

Words and Music by Carl Wright

†Albert Collins

††Symbols in parentheses represent chord names respective to capoed Gtr. 3.
Symbols above represent actual sounding chords. Capoed fret is "0" in tab.
Chord symbols reflect basic harmony.

Verse

laughed at her __ a-bout a week a-go, __ now __ she's met a man ___ with a whole __ lot - ta dough.

And, oh, __ yeah, he's rich, I've __ seen the mon - ey. All _____ she had to do was ___ to call the man, __ hon-ey, hon-

ey, hon-ey. She's in-to some-thing, __ yeah, _____ she's in - to some-thing. Man, ___

she's __ in-to some-thing, __ you should be in-to some - thing, too. __

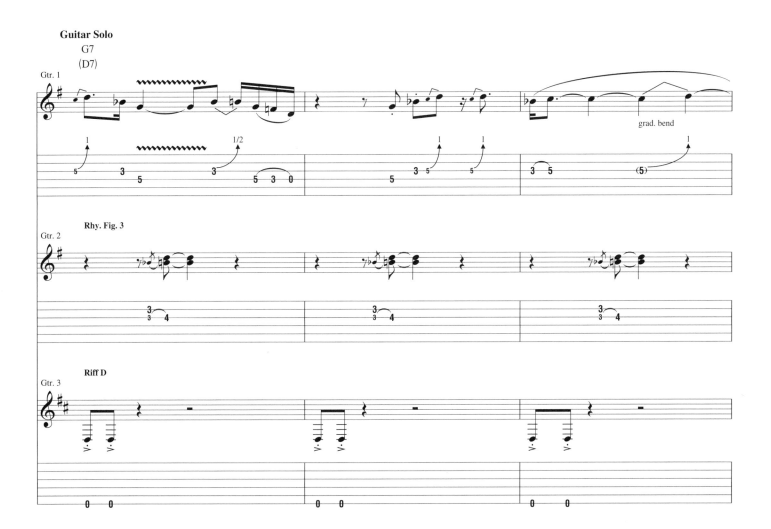

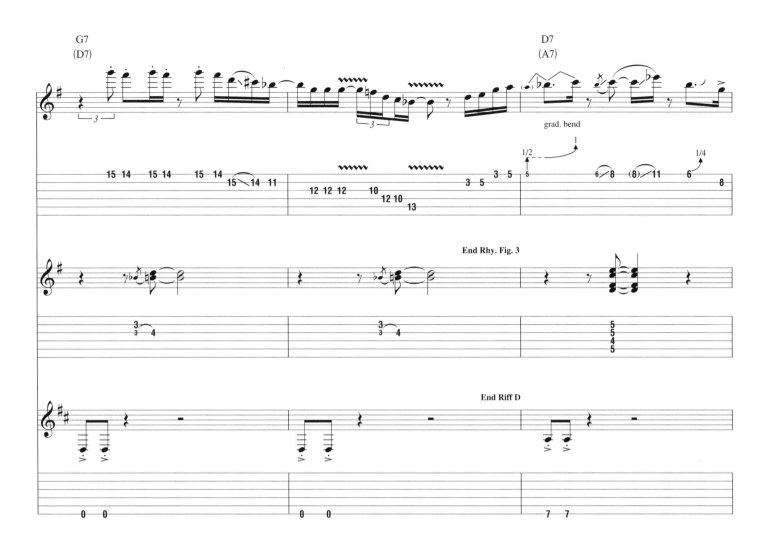

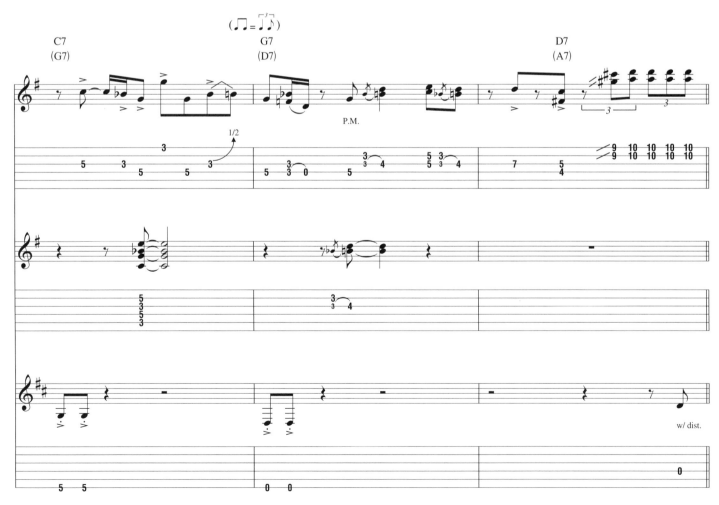

Guitar Solo

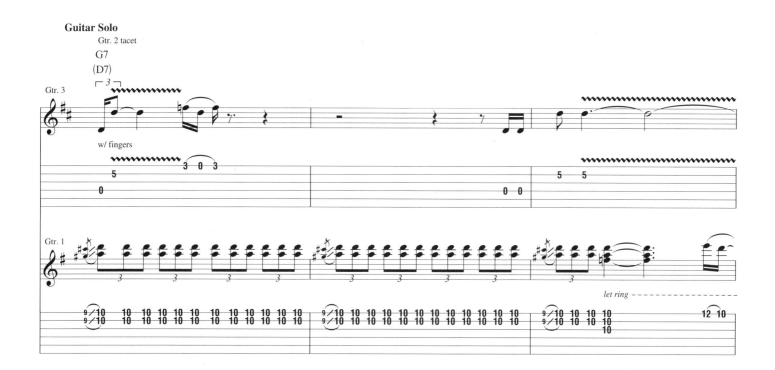

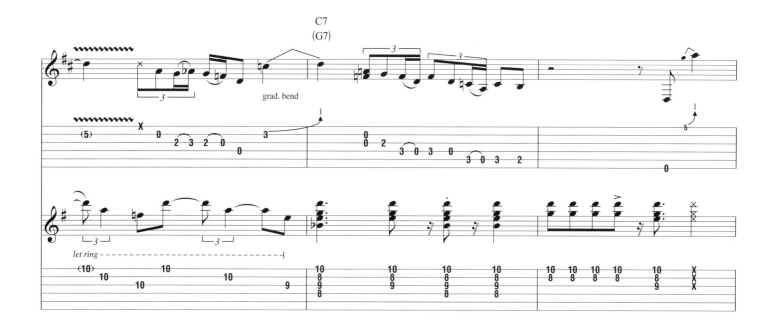

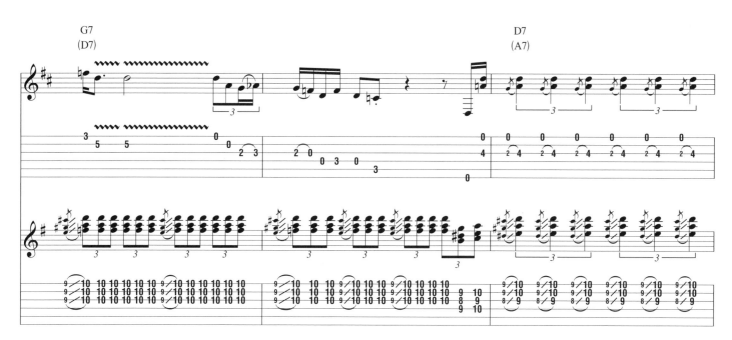

119

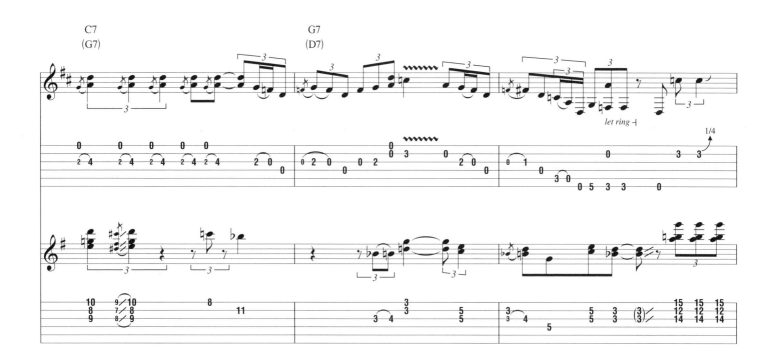

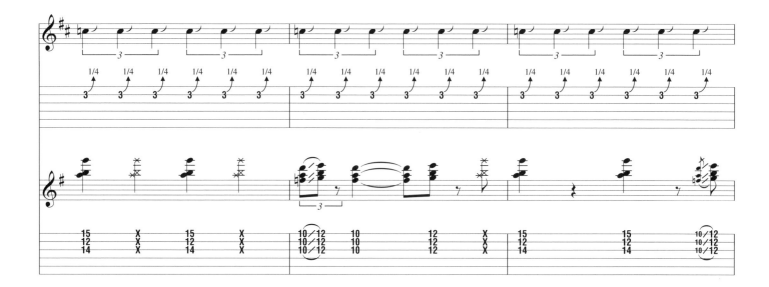

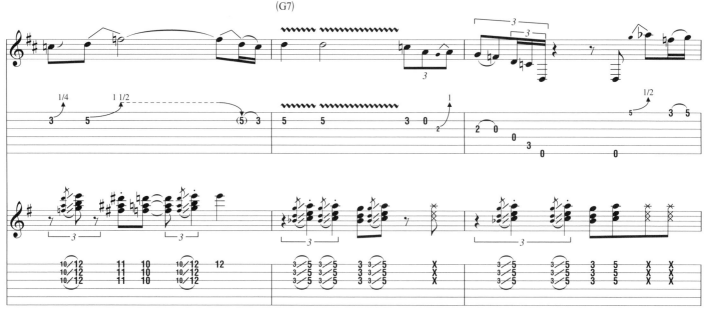

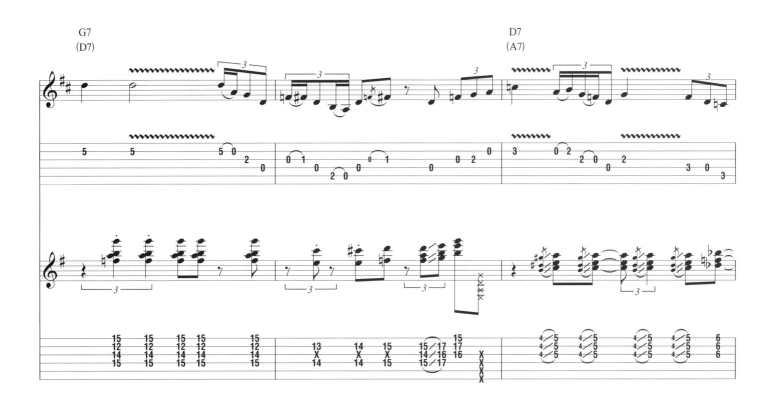

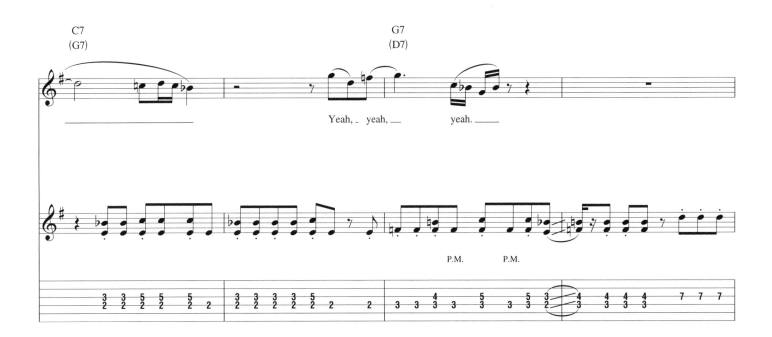

Yeah, _ yeah, _ yeah. _____

P.M.   P.M.

Gtr. 3 tacet

Say what she do!

Gtr. 1

P.M.

Gtr. 2

P.M.

from *Strong Persuader*

Smoking Gun

Words and Music by Bruce Bromberg, Richard Cousins and Robert Cray

Am   N.C.   Em

yeah. ___ And I'm so a - fraid _____ I'm gon-na find you with a so - called _ smok - in' gun. _

And I know just when _ to catch you with that well - known _ smok - in' gun. _

End Rhy. Fig. 2

let ring

|1.

Interlude

Em

Rhy. Fig. 3   **End Rhy. Fig. 3**

|2.

Interlude

Gtr. 1: w/ Rhy. Fig. 3

Em

Gtr. 2 (clean)

mf

Guitar Solo

Gtr. 1: w/ Rhy. Fig. 1 (4 times)

Em

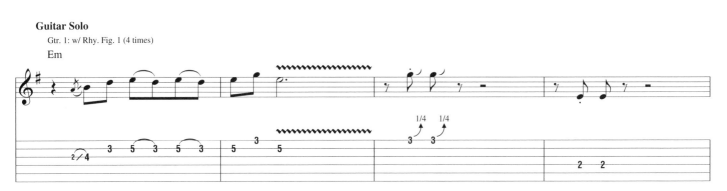

Gtr. 1: w/ Rhy. Fig. 2

Am   Em

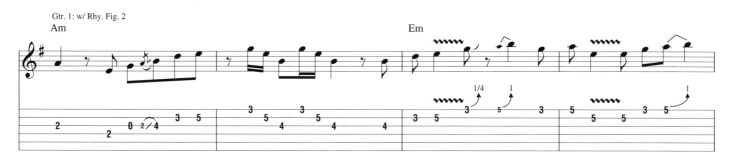

Am   N.C.   Gtr. 1: w/ Rhy. Fig. 3

                                                             Em

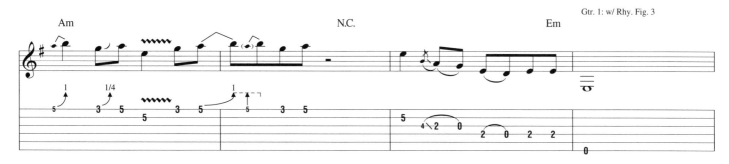

Gtr. 1: w/ Rhy. Fig. 1 (4 times)

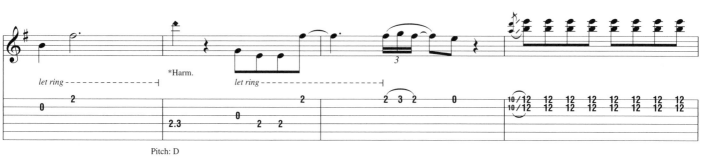

Pitch: D
*Harmonic located one third the distance between the 2nd & 3rd frets.

Gtr. 1: w/ Rhy. Fig. 2
Am

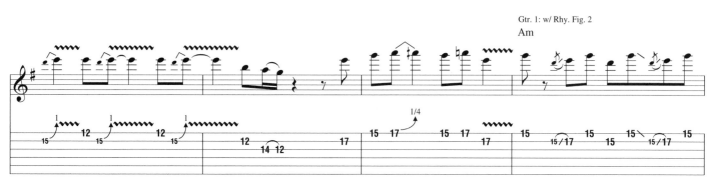

Gtr. 1: w/ Rhy. Fig. 3

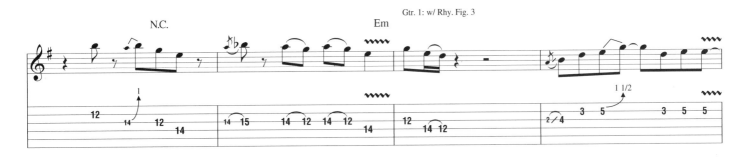

3. I'm

Verse

Gtr. 1: w/ Rhy. Fig. 1 (4 times)

stand - ing ___ here ___ be - wil - dered, I can't re - mem-ber just what ___ I've done. ___ I can

hear the si - rens ___ whin - ing, my eyes blind - ed by ___ the sun. ___ I

128

Oh, __ they've tak - en it; still __ hot smok - in' gun. __ They've

knocked me down, they've tak - en it. Oh, _____ oh, yeah. __

Ah. __

Begin fade   Fade out

from *Time Will Tell*

Time Makes Two

Words and Music by Robert Cray

*Chord symbols reflect implied harmony.

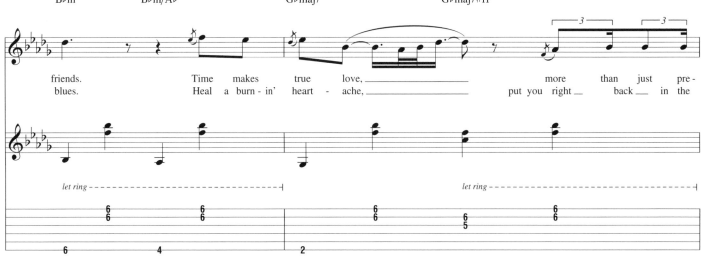

Guitar Solo

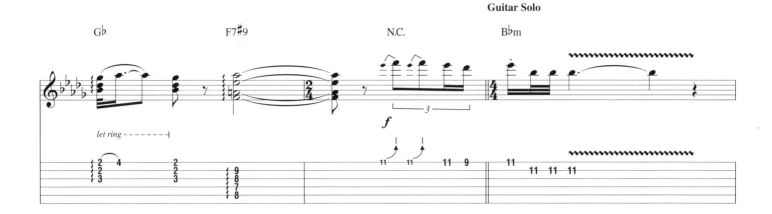

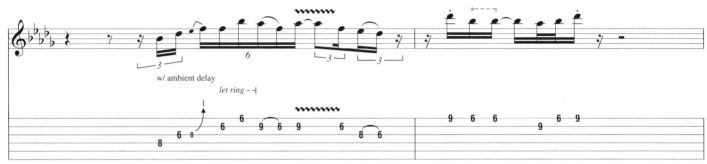

*Played ahead of the beat.

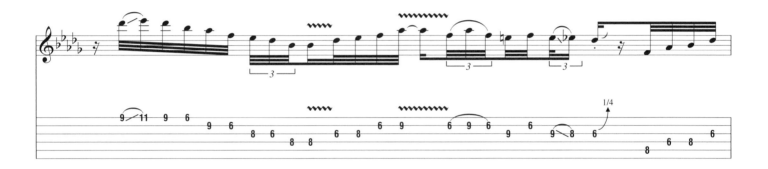

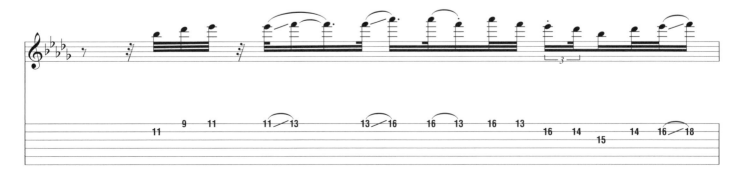

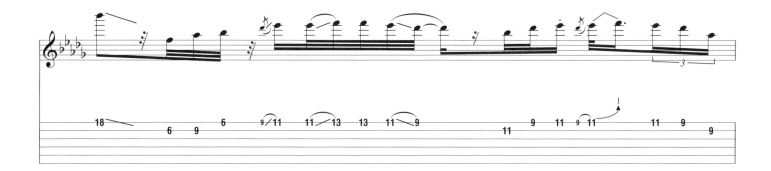

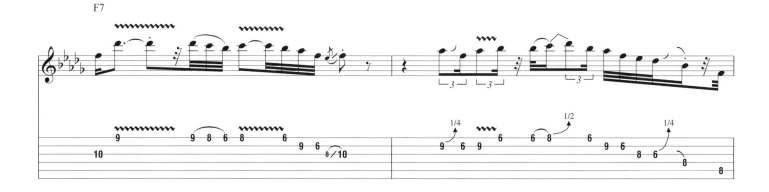

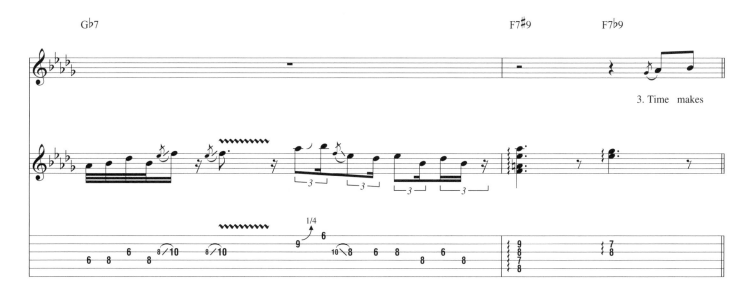

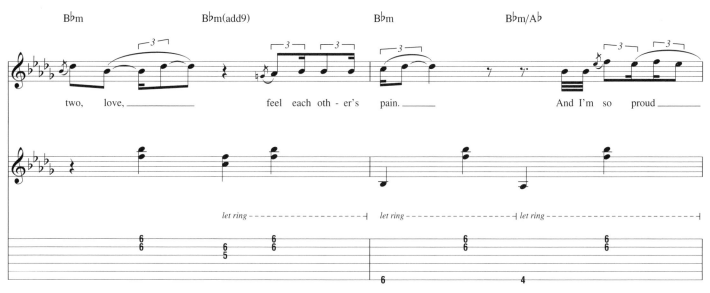

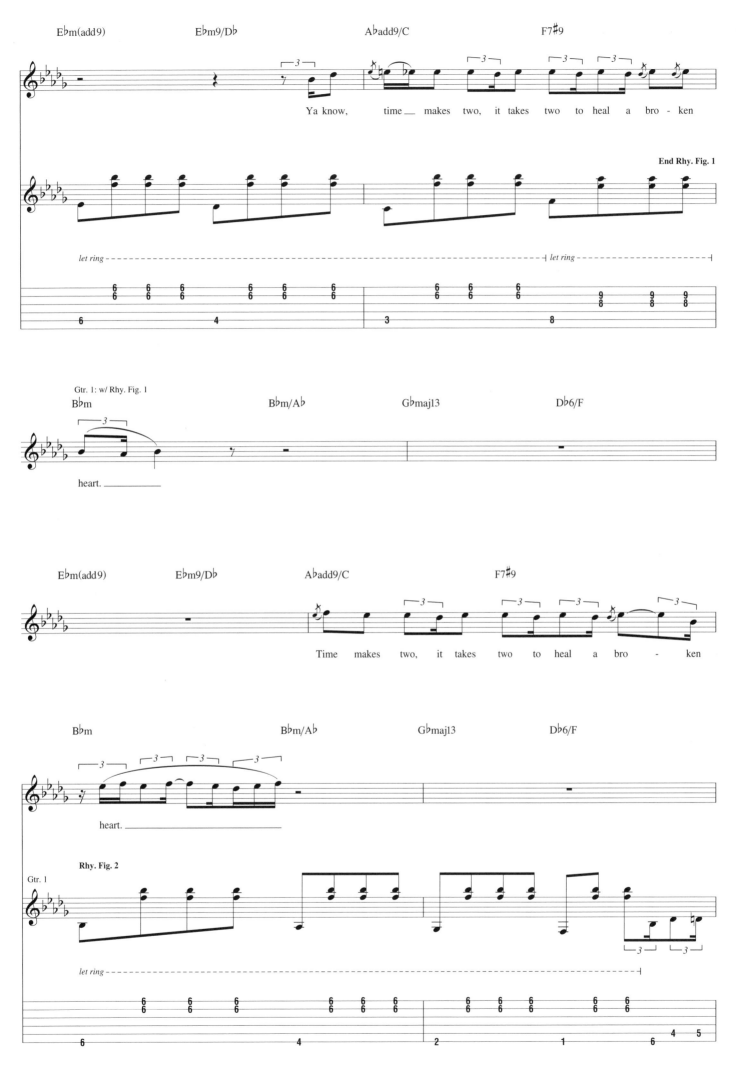

from *In My Soul*
What Would You Say
Words and Music by Robert Cray

*Composite arrangement

**Chord symbols reflect basic harmony.

Verse

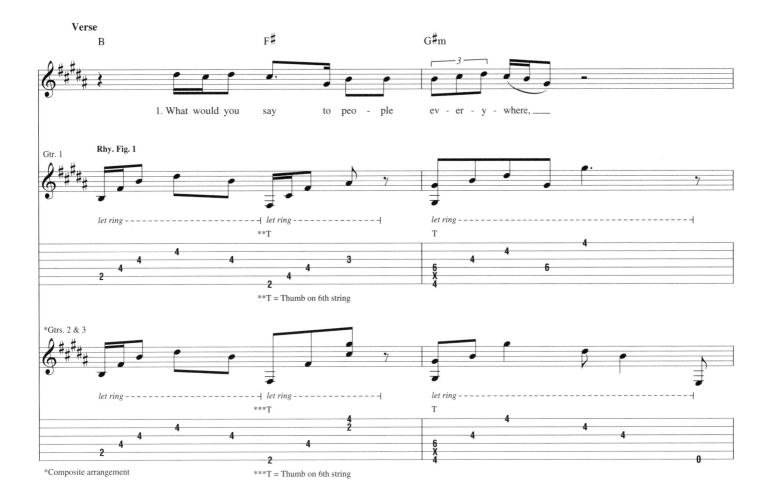

1. What would you say to peo - ple ev - er - y - where, ___

*Composite arrangement

**T = Thumb on 6th string

***T = Thumb on 6th string

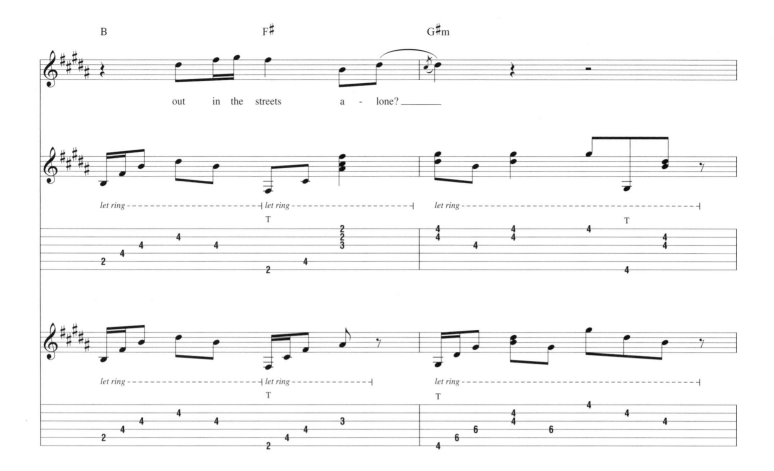

out   in   the   streets   a - lone? _____

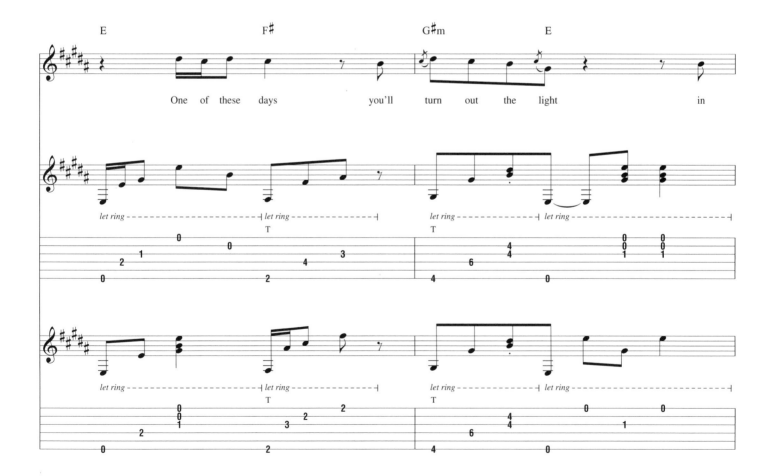

One   of   these   days   you'll   turn   out   the   light   in

some place __ to call your own. __

Gtr. 1

End Rhy. Fig. 1

let ring ------------- T ------- *let ring* ----------- *let ring* -------

Gtr. 2

let ring --------------- T ------------- *let ring* ---------------------

Gtr. 3

T -------------

%% Verse

B   F#   G#m

2. What would you   say   if we cured all __ dis - ease? __
3. What would you   say   if we quit wag - ing war __

Gtr. 1

let ring ------------------ *let ring* -----------
T   T

*Gtrs. 2 & 3

let ring ------------ *let ring* -------------- *let ring* ----------
T   T

*Composite arrangement

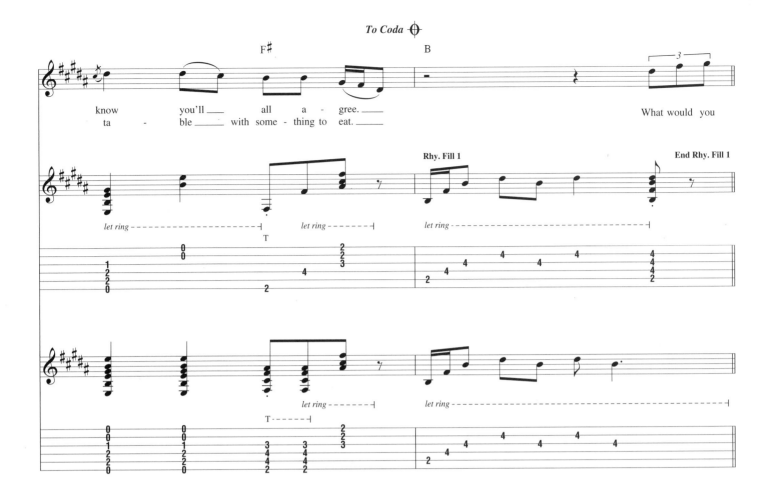

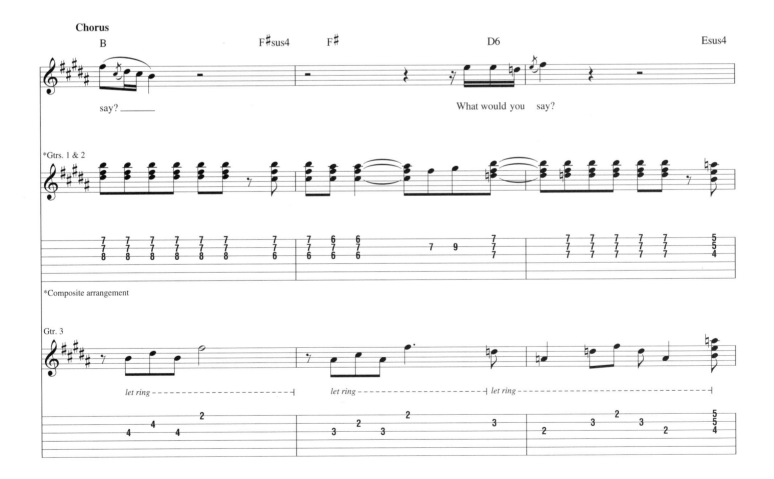

Guitar Solo

Gtr. 1: w/ Rhy. Fig. 1

*Composite arrangement

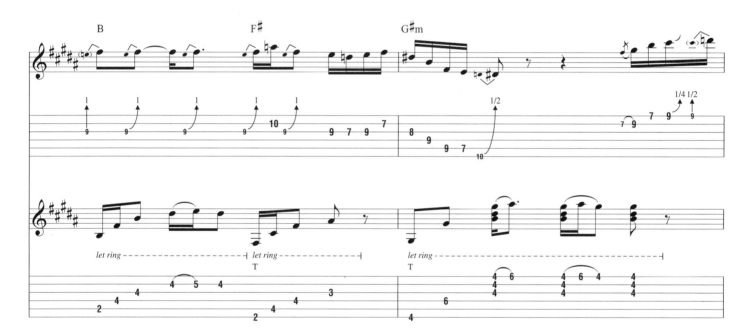

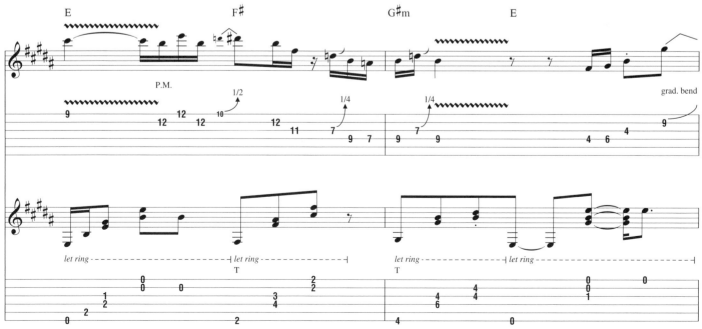

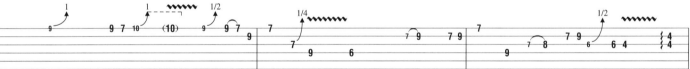

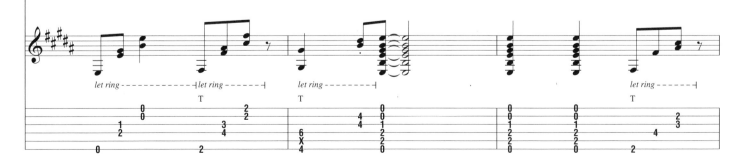

Interlude

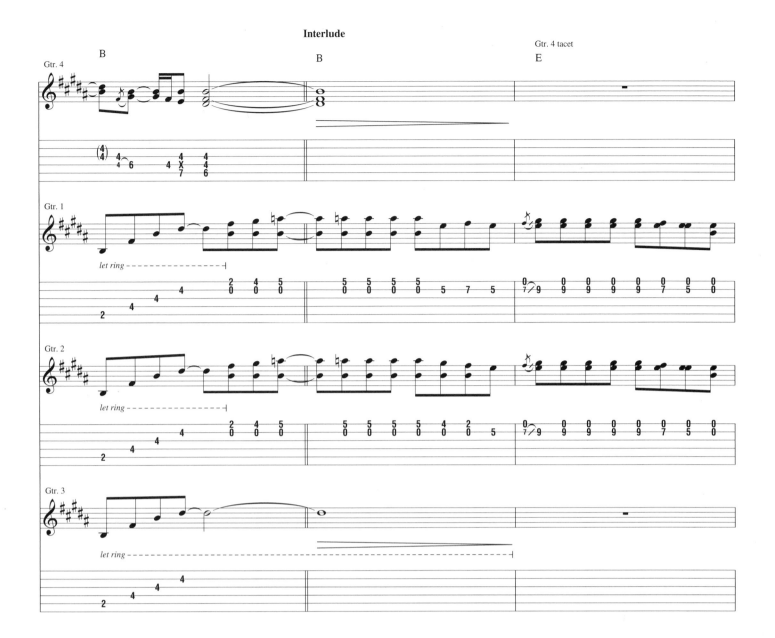

148

Coda

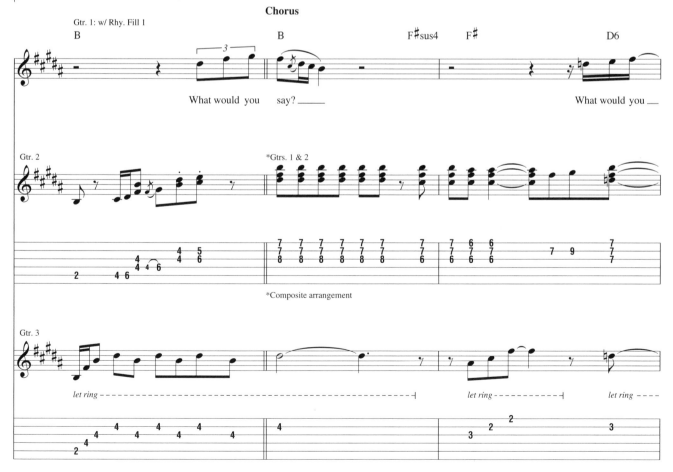

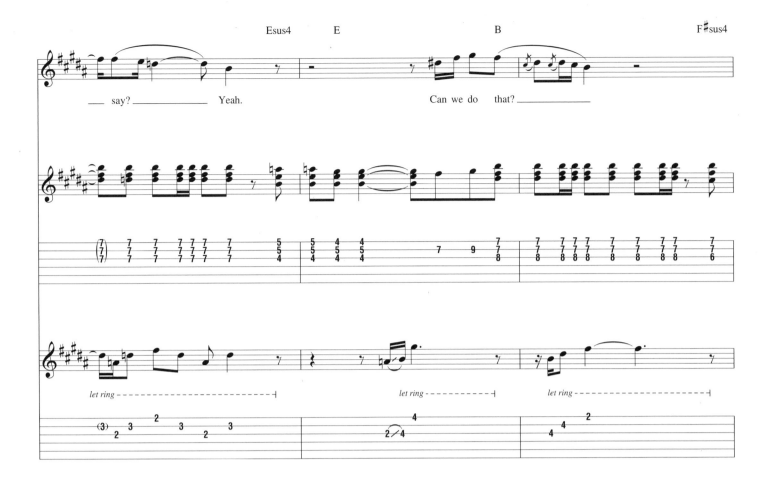

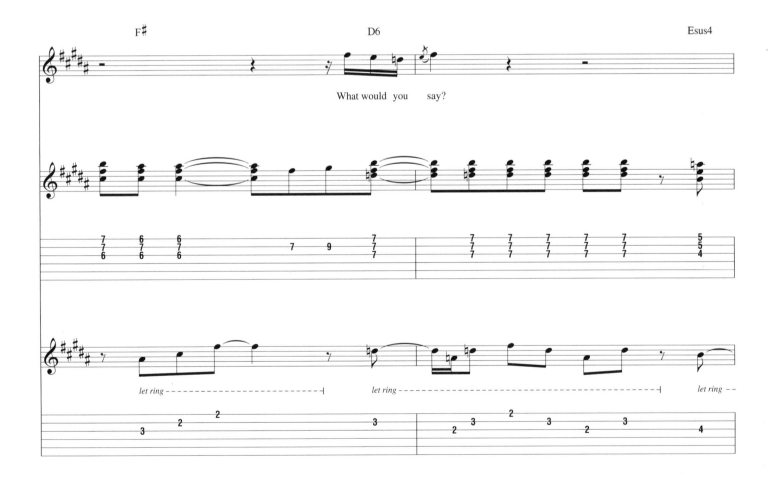

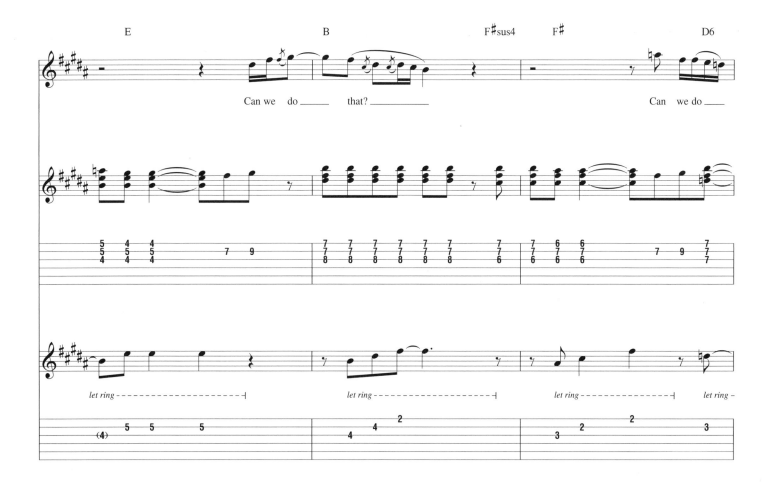

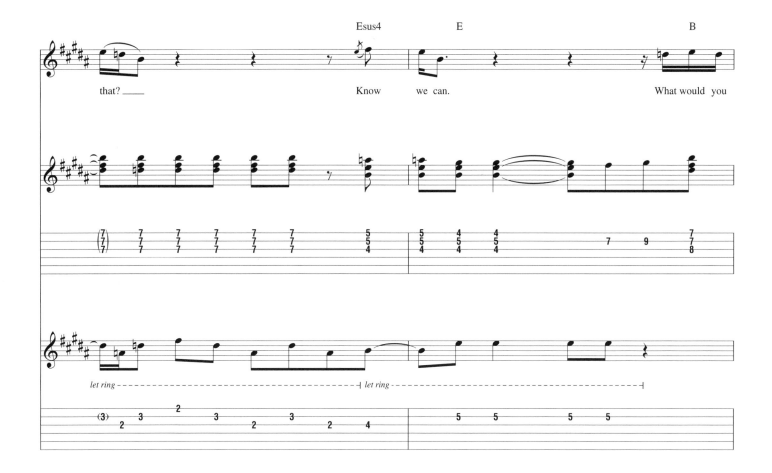

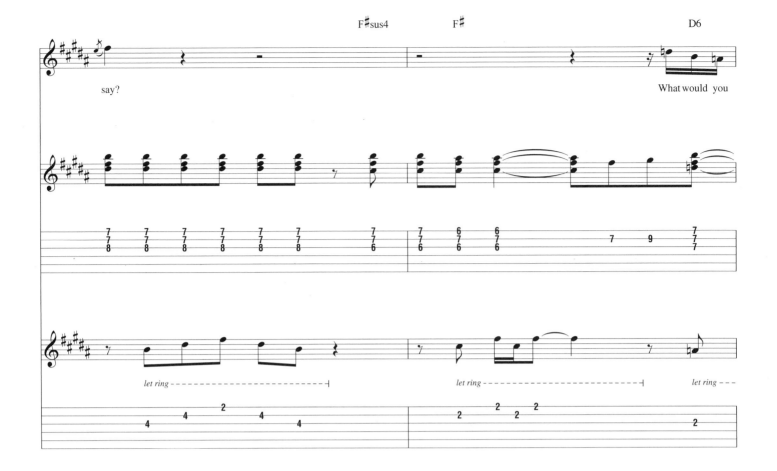

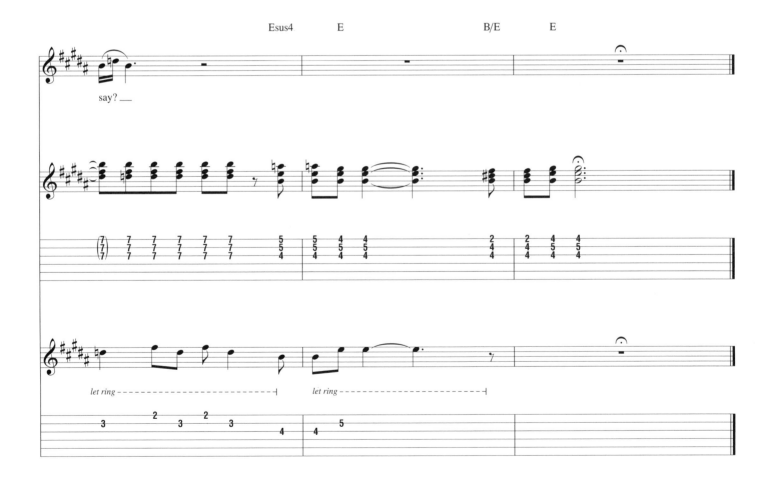

from *In My Soul*
You Move Me
Words and Music by Robert Cray

Intro
Moderately ♩ = 120

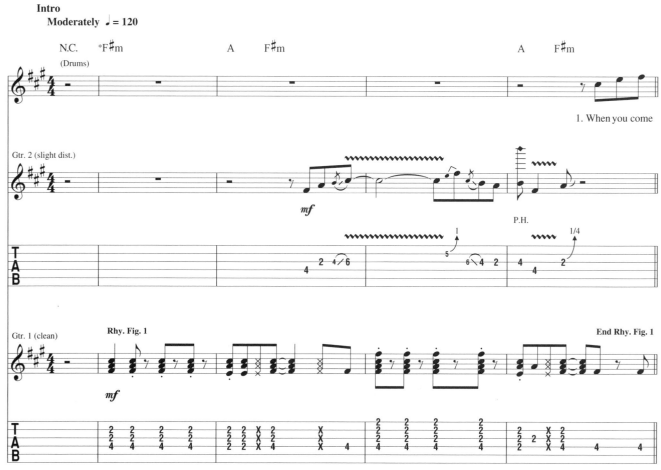

*Chord symbols reflect overall harmony.

Verse

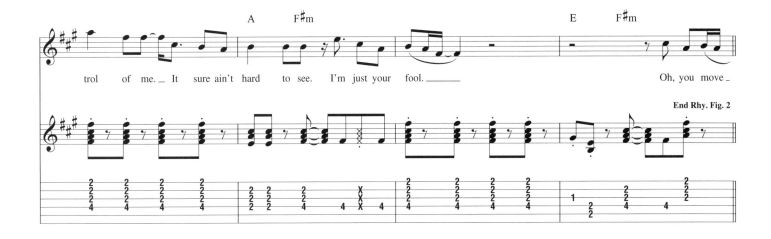

trol of me.__ It sure ain't hard to see. I'm just your fool._____ Oh, you move_

End Rhy. Fig. 2

Chorus

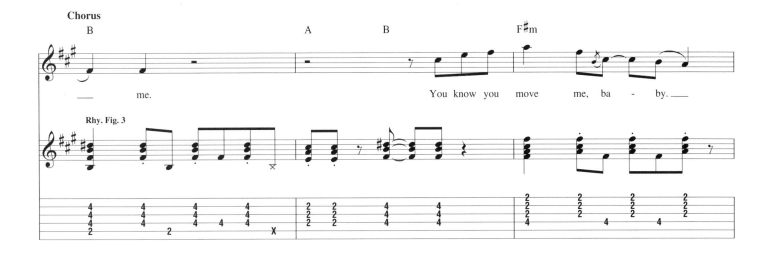

__ me. You know you move me, ba - by.__

Rhy. Fig. 3

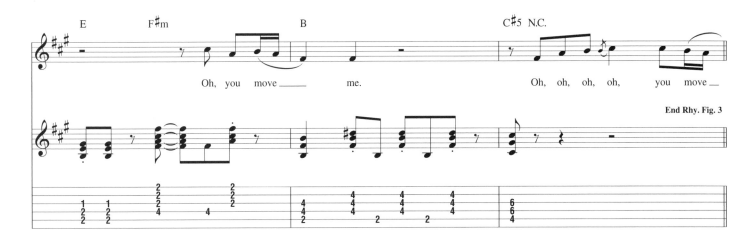

Oh, you move _____ me. Oh, oh, oh, oh, you move__

End Rhy. Fig. 3

Interlude

Gtr. 1: w/ Rhy. Fig. 1

__ me. 2. You make me

Gtr. 2

w/ pick & fingers

154

Verse

Gtr. 1: w/ Rhy. Fig. 2

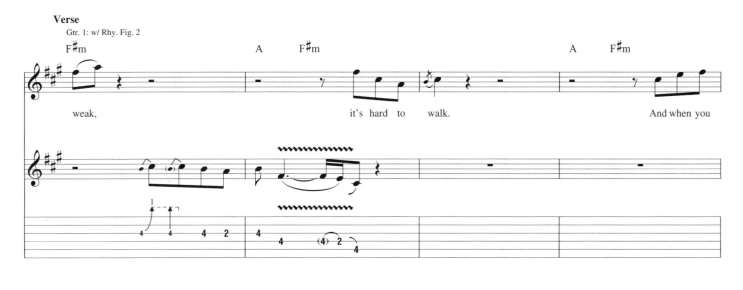

weak,   it's hard to walk.   And when you

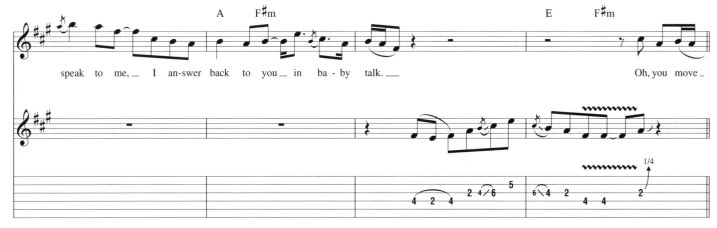

speak to me, _ I an-swer back to you _ in ba-by talk. _   Oh, you move _

Chorus

Gtr. 1: w/ Rhy. Fig. 3

_ me.   You know you move me, ba-by. _   Oh, you move _

Interlude

Gtr. 1: w/ Rhy. Fig. 1 (1st 2 meas.)

_ me.   Oh, oh, oh, oh, you move _____ me.

Guitar Solo

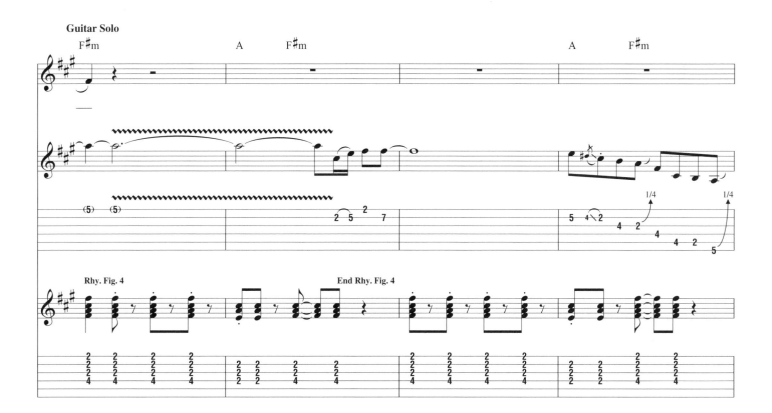

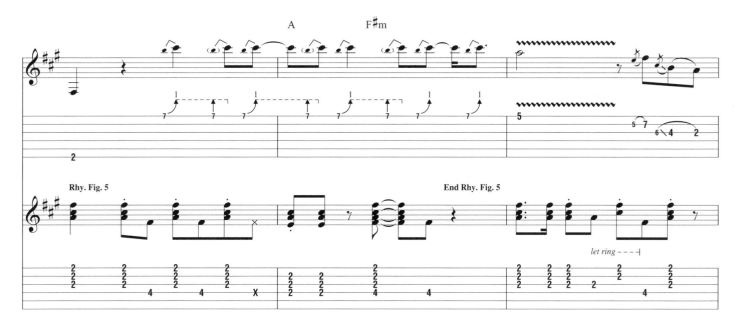

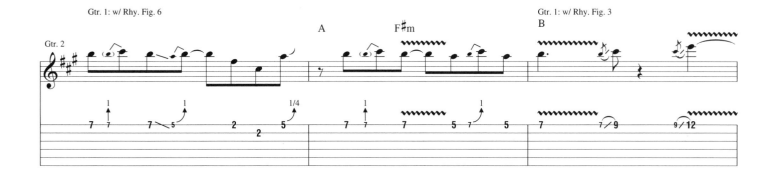

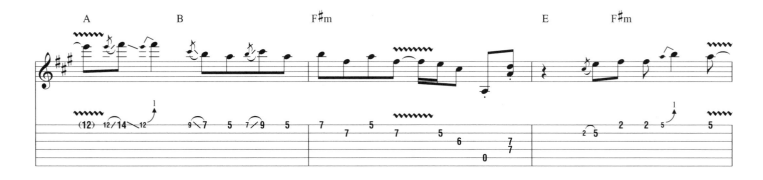

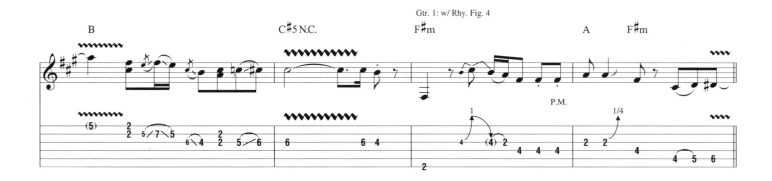

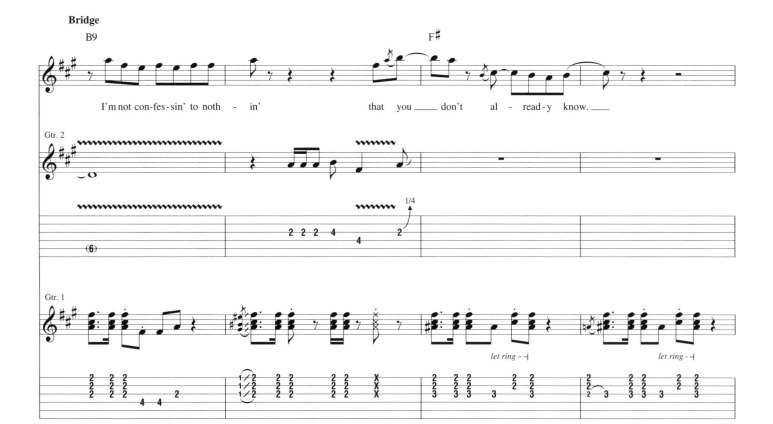

Let me tell you some - thing; — Don't you ev - er, ev - er let me go. — Oh, __ no. __

Interlude
Gtr. 1: w/ Rhy. Fig. 4

F#m   A   F#m

Verse
Gtr. 1: w/ Rhy. Fig. 5 (3 1/2 times)

F#m   A   F#m

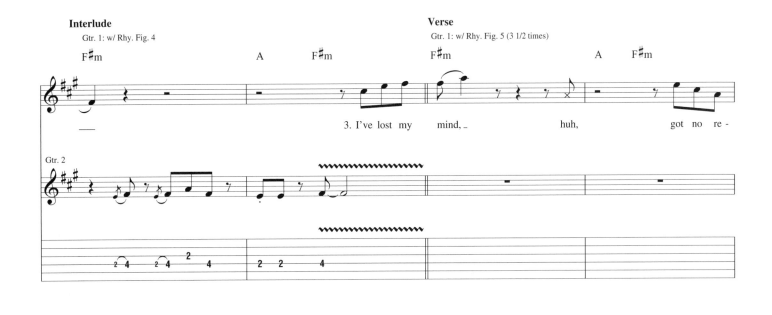

__ 3. I've lost my mind, _ huh, got no re -

Gtr. 2

A   F#m   A   F#m

grets. __ Be - cause I know for sure _ that I don't need a cure, _ you can sure - ly

P.M.

Chorus

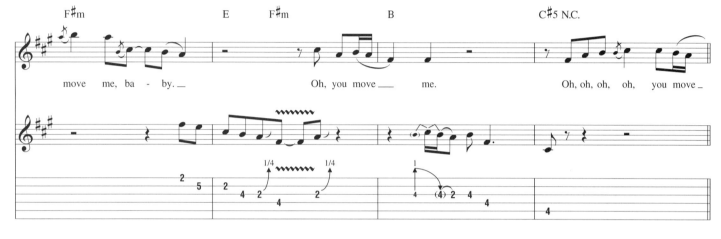

Outro-Guitar Solo

way you do your thing.   Well, it moves me, ba - by.   Ah, _____

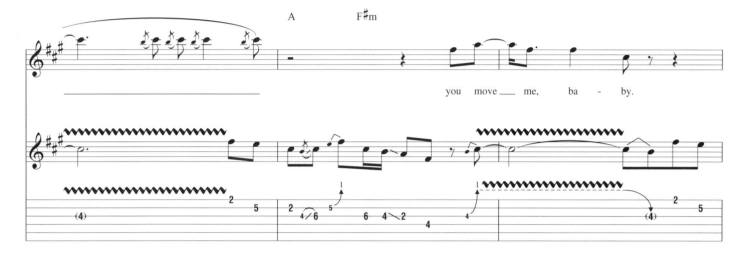

you move me, ba - by.

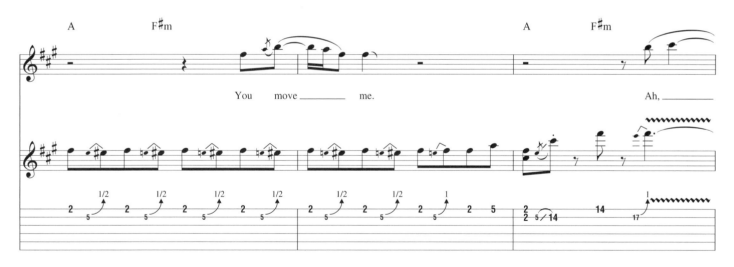

You move _____ me.   Ah, _____

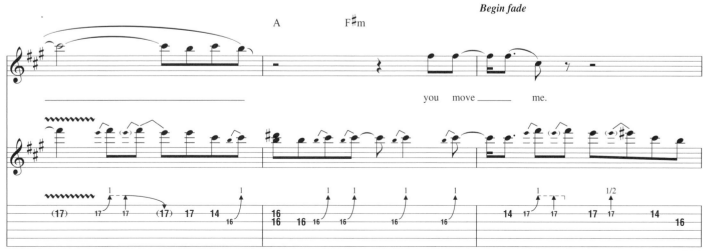

Begin fade

you move _____ me.

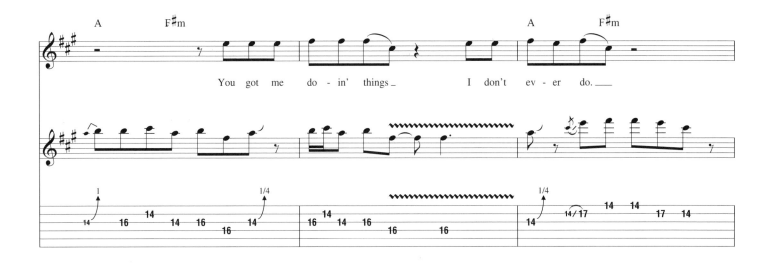

You got me do - in' things _ I don't ev - er do. ____

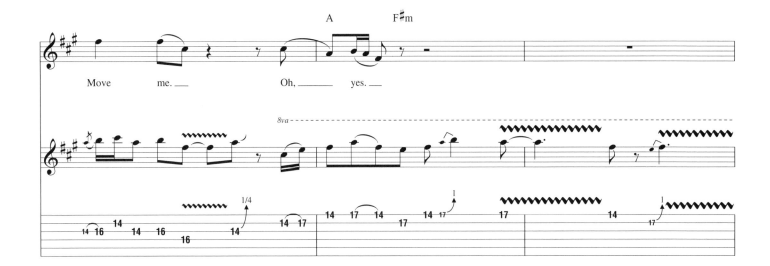

Move me. ____ Oh, ____ yes.

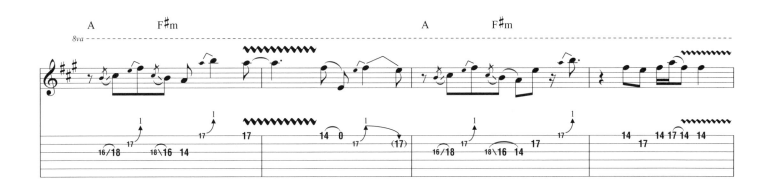

Fade out

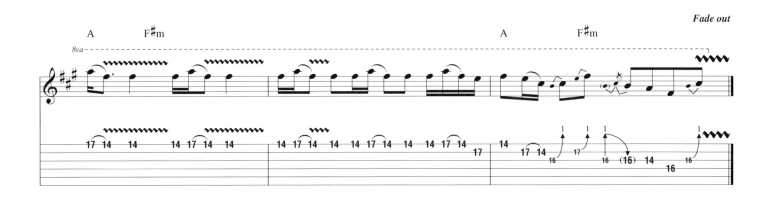

162

GUITAR NOTATION LEGEND

Guitar music can be notated three different ways: on a *musical staff*, in *tablature*, and in *rhythm slashes*.

RHYTHM SLASHES are written above the staff. Strum chords in the rhythm indicated. Use the chord diagrams found at the top of the first page of the transcription for the appropriate chord voicings. Round noteheads indicate single notes.

THE MUSICAL STAFF shows pitches and rhythms and is divided by bar lines into measures. Pitches are named after the first seven letters of the alphabet.

TABLATURE graphically represents the guitar fingerboard. Each horizontal line represents a string, and each number represents a fret.

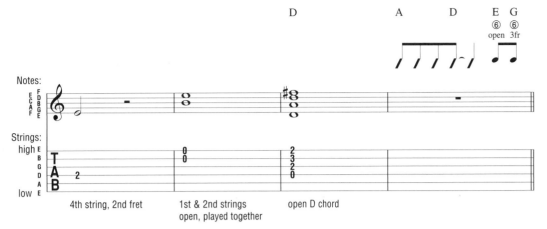

4th string, 2nd fret

1st & 2nd strings open, played together

open D chord

Definitions for Special Guitar Notation

HALF-STEP BEND: Strike the note and bend up 1/2 step.

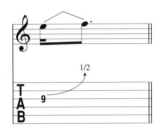

WHOLE-STEP BEND: Strike the note and bend up one step.

GRACE NOTE BEND: Strike the note and immediately bend up as indicated.

SLIGHT (MICROTONE) BEND: Strike the note and bend up 1/4 step.

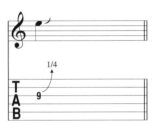

BEND AND RELEASE: Strike the note and bend up as indicated, then release back to the original note. Only the first note is struck.

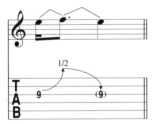

PRE-BEND: Bend the note as indicated, then strike it.

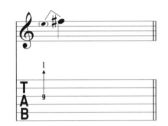

PRE-BEND AND RELEASE: Bend the note as indicated. Strike it and release the bend back to the original note.

UNISON BEND: Strike the two notes simultaneously and bend the lower note up to the pitch of the higher.

VIBRATO: The string is vibrated by rapidly bending and releasing the note with the fretting hand.

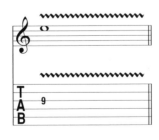

WIDE VIBRATO: The pitch is varied to a greater degree by vibrating with the fretting hand.

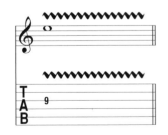

HAMMER-ON: Strike the first (lower) note with one finger, then sound the higher note (on the same string) with another finger by fretting it without picking.

PULL-OFF: Place both fingers on the notes to be sounded. Strike the first note and without picking, pull the finger off to sound the second (lower) note.

LEGATO SLIDE: Strike the first note and then slide the same fret-hand finger up or down to the second note. The second note is not struck.

SHIFT SLIDE: Same as legato slide, except the second note is struck.

TRILL: Very rapidly alternate between the notes indicated by continuously hammering on and pulling off.

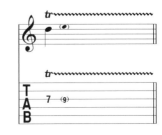

TAPPING: Hammer ("tap") the fret indicated with the pick-hand index or middle finger and pull off to the note fretted by the fret hand.

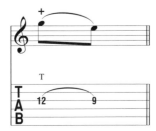

NATURAL HARMONIC: Strike the note while the fret-hand lightly touches the string directly over the fret indicated.

PINCH HARMONIC: The note is fretted normally and a harmonic is produced by adding the edge of the thumb or the tip of the index finger of the pick hand to the normal pick attack.

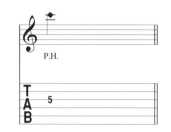

HARP HARMONIC: The note is fretted normally and a harmonic is produced by gently resting the pick hand's index finger directly above the indicated fret (in parentheses) while the pick hand's thumb or pick assists by plucking the appropriate string.

PICK SCRAPE: The edge of the pick is rubbed down (or up) the string, producing a scratchy sound.

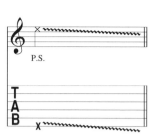

MUFFLED STRINGS: A percussive sound is produced by laying the fret hand across the string(s) without depressing, and striking them with the pick hand.

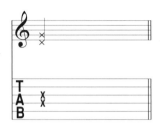

PALM MUTING: The note is partially muted by the pick hand lightly touching the string(s) just before the bridge.

RAKE: Drag the pick across the strings indicated with a single motion.

TREMOLO PICKING: The note is picked as rapidly and continuously as possible.

ARPEGGIATE: Play the notes of the chord indicated by quickly rolling them from bottom to top.

VIBRATO BAR DIVE AND RETURN: The pitch of the note or chord is dropped a specified number of steps (in rhythm), then returned to the original pitch.

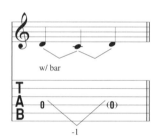

VIBRATO BAR SCOOP: Depress the bar just before striking the note, then quickly release the bar.

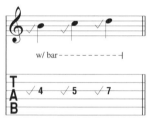

VIBRATO BAR DIP: Strike the note and then immediately drop a specified number of steps, then release back to the original pitch.

Additional Musical Definitions

> (accent)	• Accentuate note (play it louder).	
^ (accent)	• Accentuate note with great intensity.	
(staccato)	• Play the note short.	
⊓	• Downstroke	
V	• Upstroke	

D.S. al Coda • Go back to the sign (𝄋), then play until the measure marked "*To Coda*," then skip to the section labelled "**Coda**."

D.C. al Fine • Go back to the beginning of the song and play until the measure marked "*Fine*" (end).

Rhy. Fig. • Label used to recall a recurring accompaniment pattern (usually chordal).

Riff • Label used to recall composed, melodic lines (usually single notes) which recur.

Fill • Label used to identify a brief melodic figure which is to be inserted into the arrangement.

Rhy. Fill • A chordal version of a Fill.

tacet • Instrument is silent (drops out).

• Repeat measures between signs.

• When a repeated section has different endings, play the first ending only the first time and the second ending only the second time.

NOTE: Tablature numbers in parentheses mean:
1. The note is being sustained over a system (note in standard notation is tied), or
2. The note is sustained, but a new articulation (such as a hammer-on, pull-off, slide or vibrato) begins, or
3. The note is a barely audible "ghost" note (note in standard notation is also in parentheses).

MASTER THE *Blues*

With guitar instruction from Hal Leonard
All books include notes and tab.

Hal Leonard Guitar Method – Blues Guitar
by Greg Koch

The complete guide to learning blues guitar uses real blues songs to teach you the basics of rhythm and lead blues guitar in the style of B.B. King, Buddy Guy, Eric Clapton, and many others. Lessons include: 12-bar blues; chords, scales and licks; vibrato and string bending; riffs, turnarounds, and boogie patterns; and more!
00697326 Book/CD Pack $16.99

Blues Deluxe
by Dave Rubin

Not only does this deluxe edition provide accurate transcriptions of ten blues classics plus performance notes and artist bios, it also includes a CD with the *original Alligator Records recordings* of every song! Tunes: Are You Losing Your Mind? (Buddy Guy) • Don't Take Advantage of Me (Johnny Winter) • Gravel Road (Magic Slim) • Somebody Loan Me a Dime (Fenton Robinson) • and more.
00699918 Book/CD Pack $24.99

Art of the Shuffle
by Dave Rubin

This method book explores shuffle, boogie and swing rhythms for guitar. Includes tab and notation, and covers Delta, country, Chicago, Kansas City, Texas, New Orleans, West Coast, and bebop blues. Also includes audio for demonstration of each style and to jam along with.
00695005 Book/CD Pack $19.95

Power Trio Blues
by Dave Rubin

This book/CD pack details how to play electric guitar in a trio with bass and drums. Boogie, shuffle, and slow blues rhythms, licks, double stops, chords, and bass patterns are presented for full and exciting blues. A CD with the music examples performed by a smokin' power trio is included for play-along instruction and jamming.
00695028 Book/CD Pack $19.99

100 Blues Lessons
Guitar Lesson Goldmine
by John Heussenstamm and Chad Johnson

A huge variety of blues guitar styles and techniques are covered, including: turnarounds, hammer-ons and pull-offs, slides, the blues scale, 12-bar blues, double stops, muting techniques, hybrid picking, fingerstyle blues, and much more!
00696452 Book/2-CD Pack.................$24.99

Electric Slide Guitar
by David Hamburger

This book/audio method explores the basic fundamentals of slide guitar: from selecting a slide and proper setup of the guitar, to open and standard tuning. Plenty of music examples are presented showing sample licks as well as backup/rhythm slide work. Each section also examines techniques and solos in the style of the best slide guitarists, including Duane Allman, Dave Hole, Ry Cooder, Bonnie Raitt, Muddy Waters, Johnny Winter and Elmore James.
00695022 Book/CD Pack....................$19.95

101 Must-Know Blues Licks
A Quick, Easy Reference for All Guitarists
by Wolf Marshall

Now you can add authentic blues feel and flavor to your playing! Here are 101 definitive licks – plus a demonstration CD – from every major blues guitar style, neatly organized into easy-to-use categories. They're all here, including Delta blues, jump blues, country blues, Memphis blues, Texas blues, West Coast blues, Chicago blues, and British blues.
00695318 Book/CD Pack....................$17.95

Fretboard Roadmaps Blues Guitar
for Acoustic and Electric Guitar
by Fred Sokolow

These essential fretboard patterns are roadmaps that all great blues guitarists know and use. This book teaches how to: play lead and rhythm anywhere on the fretboard, in any key; play a variety of lead guitar styles; play chords and progressions anywhere on the fretboard, in any key; expand chord vocabulary; learn to think musically, the way the pros do.
00695350 Book/CD Pack....................$14.95

The Road to Robert Johnson
The Genesis and Evolution of Blues in the Delta from the Late 1800s Through 1938
by Edward Komara

This book traces the development of the legendary Robert Johnson's music in light of the people and songs that directly and indirectly influenced him. It includes much information about life in the Delta from the late 1800s to Johnson's controversial death in 1938, and features fascinating historical photos, maps, musical examples, and much more.
00695388.............................$14.95

12-Bar Blues
by Dave Rubin

The term "12-bar blues" has become synonymous with blues music and is the basis for an incredible body of jazz, rock 'n' roll, and other forms of popular music. This book/CD pack is solely devoted to providing guitarists with all the technical tools necessary for playing 12-bar blues with authority. The CD includes 24 full-band tracks. Covers: boogie, shuffle, swing, riff, and jazzy blues progressions; Chicago, minor, slow, bebop, and other blues styles; soloing, intros, turnarounds, and more.
00695187 Book/CD Pack.....................$18.99

Smokin' Blues Guitar
by Smokin' Joe Kubek with Dave Rubin

Texas blues guitar legend Smokin' Joe Kubek and acclaimed author and music historian Dave Rubin have teamed up to create this one-of-a-kind DVD/book bundle, featuring a high-definition DVD with Smokin' Joe himself demonstrating loads of electric blues licks, riffs, concepts, and techniques straight from his extensive arsenal. The companion book, co-written with Dave Rubin, provides standard notation and tablature for every smokin' example on the DVD, as well as bonus instructional material, and much more!
00696469 Book/DVD Pack $24.99

Blues You Can Use
by John Ganapes

A comprehensive source for learning blues guitar, designed to develop both your lead and rhythm playing. Covers all styles of blues, including Texas, Delta, R&B, early rock and roll, gospel, blues/rock and more. Includes 21 complete solos; extensive instruction; audio with leads and full band backing; and more!
00695007 Book/CD Pack $19.99

Blues You Can Use Chord Book
by John Ganapes

A reference guide to blues, R&B, jazz, and rock rhythm guitar, with hundreds of voicings, chord theory construction, chord progressions and exercises and much more. The Blues You Can Use Book Of Guitar Chords is useful for the beginner to advanced player.
00695082 .... $14.95

More Blues You Can Use
by John Ganapes

A complete guide to learning blues guitar, covering scales, rhythms, chords, patterns, rakes, techniques, and more. CD includes 13 full-demo solos.
00695165 Book/CD Pack $19.95

Blues Licks You Can Use
by John Ganapes

Contains music and performance notes for 75 hot lead phrases, covering styles including up-tempo and slow blues, jazz-blues, shuffle blues, swing blues and more! CD features full-band examples.
00695386 Book/CD Pack $16.95

HAL•LEONARD®
CORPORATION

7777 W. BLUEMOUND RD. P.O. BOX 13819 MILWAUKEE, WI 53213

www.halleonard.com

Prices, availability, and contents subject to change without notice. Some products may not be available outside the U.S.A.

0313

GUITAR RECORDED VERSIONS®

Guitar Recorded Versions® are note-for-note transcriptions of guitar music taken directly off recordings. This series, one of the most popular in print today, features some of the greatest guitar players and groups from blues and rock to country and jazz.

Guitar Recorded Versions are transcribed by the best transcribers in the business. Every book contains notes and tablature. Visit www.halleonard.com for our complete selection.

AUTHENTIC TRANSCRIPTIONS WITH NOTES AND TABLATURE

00690169 Eric Johnson – Venus Isle $22.95
00122439 Jack Johnson – From Here to Now to You $22.99
00690846 Jack Johnson and Friends – Sing-A-Longs and Lullabies for the Film Curious George $19.95
00690271 Robert Johnson – The New Transcriptions $24.95
00699131 Best of Janis Joplin $19.95
00690427 Best of Judas Priest $22.99
00690277 Best of Kansas $19.95
00690911 Best of Phil Keaggy $24.99
00690727 Toby Keith Guitar Collection $19.99
00120814 Killswitch Engage – Disarm the Descent $22.99
00690504 Very Best of Albert King $19.95
00690444 B.B. King & Eric Clapton – Riding with the King $22.99
00690134 Freddie King Collection $19.95
00691062 Kings of Leon – Come Around Sundown $22.99
00690157 Kiss – Alive! $19.95
00690356 Kiss – Alive II $22.99
00694903 Best of Kiss for Guitar $24.95
00690355 Kiss – Destroyer $16.95
14026320 Mark Knopfler – Get Lucky $22.99
00690164 Mark Knopfler Guitar – Vol. 1 $19.95
00690163 Mark Knopfler/Chet Atkins – Neck and Neck $19.95
00690780 Korn – Greatest Hits, Volume 1 $22.95
00690377 Kris Kristofferson Collection $19.95
00690834 Lamb of God – Ashes of the Wake $19.95
00690875 Lamb of God – Sacrament $19.95
00690977 Ray LaMontagne – Gossip in the Grain $19.99
00690823 Ray LaMontagne – Trouble $19.95
00691057 Ray LaMontagne and the Pariah Dogs – God Willin' & The Creek Don't Rise $22.99
00690781 Linkin Park – Hybrid Theory $22.95
00690782 Linkin Park – Meteora $22.95
00690922 Linkin Park – Minutes to Midnight $19.95
00699623 The Best of Chuck Loeb $19.95
00114563 The Lumineers $22.99
00690525 Best of George Lynch $24.99
00690955 Lynyrd Skynyrd – All-Time Greatest Hits $19.99
00694954 New Best of Lynyrd Skynyrd $19.95
00690577 Yngwie Malmsteen – Anthology $24.95
00690754 Marilyn Manson – Lest We Forget $19.95
00694956 Bob Marley – Legend $19.95
00690548 Very Best of Bob Marley & The Wailers – One Love $22.99
00694945 Bob Marley – Songs of Freedom $24.95
00690914 Maroon 5 – It Won't Be Soon Before Long $19.95
00690657 Maroon 5 – Songs About Jane $19.95
00690748 Maroon 5 – 1.22.03 Acoustic $19.95
00690989 Mastodon – Crack the Skye $22.99
00119220 Brent Mason – Hot Wired $19.99
00691176 Mastodon – The Hunter $22.99
00690616 Matchbox Twenty – More Than You Think You Are $19.95
00690239 Matchbox 20 – Yourself or Someone like You $19.95
00691942 Andy McKee – Art of Motion $22.99
00691034 Andy McKee – Joyland $19.99
00690382 Sarah McLachlan – Mirrorball $19.95
00120080 The Don McLean Songbook $19.95
00694952 Megadeth – Countdown to Extinction $22.95
00690244 Megadeth – Cryptic Writings $19.95
00694951 Megadeth – Rust in Peace $22.95
00690011 Megadeth – Youthanasia $19.95
00690505 John Mellencamp Guitar Collection $19.95
00690562 Pat Metheny – Bright Size Life $19.95
00691073 Pat Metheny with Christian McBride & Antonion Sanchez – Day Trip/Tokyo Day Trip Live $22.99
00690646 Pat Metheny – One Quiet Night $19.95
00690559 Pat Metheny – Question & Answer $19.95
00118836 Pat Metheny – Unity Band $22.99
00102590 Pat Metheny – What's It All About $22.99
00690040 Steve Miller Band Greatest Hits $19.95
00119338 Ministry Guitar Tab Collection $24.99
00690769 Modest Mouse – Good News for People Who Love Bad News $19.95
00102591 Wes Montgomery Guitar Anthology $24.99
00694802 Gary Moore – Still Got the Blues $22.99
00691005 Best of Motion City Soundtrack $19.99
00690787 Mudvayne – L.D. 50 $22.95
00691070 Mumford & Sons – Sigh No More $22.99
00118196 Muse – The 2nd Law $19.99
00690996 My Morning Jacket Collection $19.99
00690984 Matt Nathanson – Some Mad Hope $22.99
00690611 Nirvana $22.95
00694895 Nirvana – Bleach $19.95
00694913 Nirvana – In Utero $19.95
00694883 Nirvana – Nevermind $19.95
00690026 Nirvana – Unplugged in New York $19.95
00120112 No Doubt – Tragic Kingdom $22.95
00690226 Oasis – The Other Side of Oasis $19.95
00307163 Oasis – Time Flies... 1994-2009 $19.99
00690818 The Best of Opeth $22.95
00691052 Roy Orbison – Black & White Night $22.99
00694847 Best of Ozzy Osbourne $22.95
00690399 Ozzy Osbourne – The Ozzman Cometh $22.99
00690129 Ozzy Osbourne – Ozzmosis $22.95
00690933 Best of Brad Paisley $22.95
00690995 Brad Paisley – Play: The Guitar Album $24.99
00690939 Christopher Parkening – Solo Pieces $19.99
00690594 Best of Les Paul $19.95
00694855 Pearl Jam – Ten $22.99
00690439 A Perfect Circle – Mer De Noms $19.95
00690725 Best of Carl Perkins $19.99
00690499 Tom Petty – Definitive Guitar Collection $19.95
00690868 Tom Petty – Highway Companion $19.95
00690176 Phish – Billy Breathes $22.95
00691249 Phish – Junta $22.99
00690428 Pink Floyd – Dark Side of the Moon $19.95
00690789 Best of Poison $19.95
00690299 Best of Elvis: The King of Rock 'n' Roll $19.95
00692535 Elvis Presley $19.95
00690925 The Very Best of Prince $22.99
00690003 Classic Queen $24.95
00694975 Queen – Greatest Hits $24.95
00690670 Very Best of Queensryche $19.95
00690878 The Raconteurs – Broken Boy Soldiers $19.95
00109303 Radiohead Guitar Anthology $24.99
00694910 Rage Against the Machine $19.95
00119834 Rage Against the Machine – Guitar Anthology $22.99
00690179 Rancid – And Out Come the Wolves $22.95
00690426 Best of Ratt $19.95
00690055 Red Hot Chili Peppers – Blood Sugar Sex Magik $19.95
00690584 Red Hot Chili Peppers – By the Way $19.95
00690379 Red Hot Chili Peppers – Californication $19.95
00690673 Red Hot Chili Peppers – Greatest Hits $19.95
00690090 Red Hot Chili Peppers – One Hot Minute $22.95
00691166 Red Hot Chili Peppers – I'm with You $22.99
00690852 Red Hot Chili Peppers – Stadium Arcadium $24.95
00690511 Django Reinhardt – The Definitive Collection $19.95
00690779 Relient K – MMHMM $19.95
00690643 Relient K – Two Lefts Don't Make a Right ... But Three Do $19.95
00690260 Jimmie Rodgers Guitar Collection $19.95
14041901 Rodrigo Y Gabriela and C.U.B.A. – Area 52 $24.99
00690014 Rolling Stones – Exile on Main Street $24.95
00690631 Rolling Stones – Guitar Anthology $27.95
00690685 David Lee Roth – Eat 'Em and Smile $19.95
00690031 Santana's Greatest Hits $19.95
00690796 Very Best of Michael Schenker $19.95
00690566 Best of Scorpions $22.95
00690604 Bob Seger – Guitar Anthology $19.95
00691012 Shadows Fall – Retribution $22.99
00690803 Best of Kenny Wayne Shepherd Band $19.95
00690750 Kenny Wayne Shepherd – The Place You're In $19.95
00690857 Shinedown – Us and Them $19.95
00122218 Skillet – Rise $22.99
00690872 Slayer – Christ Illusion $19.95
00690813 Slayer – Guitar Collection $19.95
00690419 Slipknot $19.95
00690973 Slipknot – All Hope Is Gone $22.99
00690330 Social Distortion – Live at the Roxy $19.95
00120004 Best of Steely Dan $24.95
00694921 Best of Steppenwolf $22.95
00690655 Best of Mike Stern $19.95
14041588 Cat Stevens – Tea for the Tillerman $19.99
00690949 Rod Stewart Guitar Anthology $19.99
00690021 Sting – Fields of Gold $19.95
00690520 Styx Guitar Collection $19.95
00120081 Sublime $19.95
00690992 Sublime – Robbin' the Hood $19.99
00690519 SUM 41 – All Killer No Filler $19.95
00691072 Best of Supertramp $22.99
00690994 Taylor Swift $22.99
00690993 Taylor Swift – Fearless $22.99
00115957 Taylor Swift – Red $21.99
00691063 Taylor Swift – Speak Now $22.99
00690767 Switchfoot – The Beautiful Letdown $19.95
00690531 System of a Down – Toxicity $19.95

RECORDED VERSIONS GUITAR®

AUTHENTIC TRANSCRIPTIONS WITH NOTES AND TABLATURE

00694824 Best of James Taylor $17.99
00694887 Best of Thin Lizzy $19.95
00690871 Three Days Grace – One-X $19.95
00690891 30 Seconds to Mars – A Beautiful Lie $19.95
00690233 The Merle Travis Collection $19.99
00690683 Robin Trower – Bridge of Sighs $19.95
00699191 U2 – Best of: 1980-1990 $19.95
00690732 U2 – Best of: 1990-2000 $19.95
00690894 U2 – 18 Singles $19.95
00690039 Steve Vai – Alien Love Secrets $24.95
00690172 Steve Vai – Fire Garden $24.95
00660137 Steve Vai – Passion & Warfare $24.95
00690881 Steve Vai – Real Illusions: Reflections $24.95
00694904 Steve Vai – Sex and Religion $24.95
00110385 Steve Vai – The Story of Light $22.99
00690392 Steve Vai – The Ultra Zone $19.95
00700555 Van Halen – Van Halen $19.99
00690024 Stevie Ray Vaughan – Couldn't Stand the Weather $19.95
00690370 Stevie Ray Vaughan and Double Trouble – The Real Deal: Greatest Hits Volume 2 $22.95
00690116 Stevie Ray Vaughan – Guitar Collection $24.95
00660136 Stevie Ray Vaughan – In Step $19.95
00694879 Stevie Ray Vaughan – In the Beginning $19.95
00660058 Stevie Ray Vaughan – Lightnin' Blues '83-'87 $24.95
00690036 Stevie Ray Vaughan – Live Alive $24.95
00694835 Stevie Ray Vaughan – The Sky Is Crying $22.95
00690025 Stevie Ray Vaughan – Soul to Soul $19.95
00690015 Stevie Ray Vaughan – Texas Flood $19.95
00690772 Velvet Revolver – Contraband $22.95
00109770 Volbeat Guitar Collection $22.99
00121808 Volbeat – Outlaw Gentlemen & Shady Ladies $22.99
00690132 The T-Bone Walker Collection $19.95
00694789 Muddy Waters – Deep Blues $24.95
00690071 Weezer (The Blue Album) $19.95
00690516 Weezer (The Green Album) $19.95
00690286 Weezer – Pinkerton $19.95
00691046 Weezer – Rarities Edition $22.99
00117511 Whitesnake Guitar Collection $19.99
00690447 Best of the Who $24.95
00691941 The Who – Acoustic Guitar Collection $22.99
00691006 Wilco Guitar Collection $22.99
00690672 Best of Dar Williams $19.95
00691017 Wolfmother – Cosmic Egg $22.99
00690319 Stevie Wonder – Some of the Best $17.95
00690596 Best of the Yardbirds $19.95
00690844 Yellowcard – Lights and Sounds $19.95
00690916 The Best of Dwight Yoakam $19.95
00691020 Neil Young – After the Goldrush $22.99
00691019 Neil Young – Everybody Knows This Is Nowhere $19.99
00690904 Neil Young – Harvest $29.99
00691021 Neil Young – Harvest Moon $22.99
00690905 Neil Young – Rust Never Sleeps $19.99
00690443 Frank Zappa – Hot Rats $19.95
00690624 Frank Zappa and the Mothers of Invention – One Size Fits All $22.99
00690623 Frank Zappa – Over-Nite Sensation $22.99
00121684 ZZ Top – Early Classics $24.99
00690589 ZZ Top – Guitar Anthology $24.95
00690960 ZZ Top Guitar Classics $19.99

HAL•LEONARD® CORPORATION
7777 W. Bluemound Rd. P.O. Box 13819 Milwaukee, WI 53213

Complete songlists and more at **www.halleonard.com**

Prices, contents, and availability subject to change without notice.